I would like to recommerok, The Satisfied Life. In all m ; is the biggest problem in peop not satisfied. How many truly (....led people do you know today? ı would venture to say not many. But, as believers, a satisfied life is not only available to each and every one of us, it is also more than possible to achieve.

For me, I find that it comes down to one simple and poignant question that you'll be asked in this book: What do you believe? Most people don't know what they believe; they believe what someone else believes. So I ask you to get into this book and really study it out. And, guess what? You'll not only redefine your life, but you'll also find out what you believe. And once you find out what you believe, then reaching your destiny and your destination in this life will be an easy thing to accomplish. Now that is a satisfied life! I highly recommend this book.

— Jesse Duplantis

My friend, Dennis Burke, is an excellent teacher of the Word. In his latest book, The Satisfied Life, he has outlined God's wonderful blueprint – one on which every believer can build a great life – a life leading to fulfillment, to purpose, to joy and contentment. He shares how to obtain the "good life" God has prepared for each of us (according to Ephesians 2:10 Amplified Bible).

What would you change in your life? Are you satisfied in every area? If not, this is the book for you. God has ordained your life to be spectacular and to demonstrate the glory, the greatness and the goodness of our Lord and Savior Jesus Christ. Study every page and then get ready to live life better than you've ever imagined!

— Jerry Savelle

I have read every page of Dennis Burke's new book *The Satisfied Life,* and I am sure it's Dennis' best book so far. Creatively written and fun to read, each page reveals truth presented in a captivating style that made me want to turn each page to see what the next page held for me. If you're looking for more — *if you desire to have a rich and satisfying life* — then I cheer you on as you read *The Satisfied Life.* It will inspire, motivate, and help you in your journey!

— *Rick Renner*
Senior Pastor
Moscow Good News Church

As a pastor I watch so many Christians who simply 'exist' when Jesus died so they could live an abundant life.

Dennis Burke's new book *The Satisfied Life,* is a must read. "Stop enduring life and start enjoying life!"

— *Jim Frease*

I believe this is the best book you have ever written and your style of writing has changed. It grabs the attention like never before. It starts the reader at a beginning point and brings them down a path of explosive revelation and reaching the goal of impartation that declares "Yes I can and will do this because God has provided it for me!!" Truly God's defining us based on the potential of what He can be in us, and what He can do through us frees us to step into a whole new future. Clear, concise, and accurately defined, this book is an absolute must read for all to step into the future God has ordained for them. Thanks for writing this Dennis.

Pastor Bob Raimondo
New Life Family Worship
Punta Gorda, Florida

THE SATISFIED LIFE

Secrets for Redefining Your Life

by

DR. DENNIS BURKE

The Satisfied Life
ISBN 978-1-936314-04-1
© 2012 by Dennis Burke
P. O. Box 150043
Arlington, TX 76015

Published by Word & Spirit Publishing
P.O. Box 701403
Tulsa, OK 74170
wordandspiritpublishing.com

Text Design and Layout:
Lisa Simpson/SimpsonProductions.net

Contents

Foreword by
Kenneth Copeland

Psalm 91:16, "With long life will I satisfy him and show him my salvation." A long, satisfied life is God's plan for His people. Why then do so many Christian people go through so much trouble, coming out of one attack of the devil into another? Let's look at a real eye opener. First Corinthians 12:18, "But now hath God set the members every one of them in the body, as it hath pleased him." Notice "every one of them." God has a plan and a place for every member of His family and a road to get to that place. That's where the satisfaction of life is. That's your special place. It's prepared and planned for that purpose. I am convinced that most of the trouble and heartache people experience comes from being on the wrong road going someplace that God did not plan for them.

What if you asked directions to the place where a great Holy Ghost meeting was going on and God's presence and power was being manifested? The directions were go down this road 10 miles and turn right. Go about 10 more miles and you'll see a big crowd of people. However, you went 10 miles and turned left instead of right. You went the 10 miles down that road and sure enough, there was a big crowd of people. So you drove straight into what you expected to be an outpouring of Jesus' love and grace, only to find out it was a huge war between two rival gangs. You're in big trouble. It's an outpouring all right—but not from God. How did I ever get into this?! By not paying better attention to directions.

This wonderful book by Dennis Burke comes out of many victorious years of following God's directions and living in the place God has planned for his and Vikki's lives and ministry. I know. Gloria and I have watched them do it right from the very beginning.

This is a powerful tool. Study it. Meditate on it. Your place of grace and your prepared road to get there is ready and waiting. You will enjoy life and enjoy it more abundantly. Jesus said so!

BE BLESSED!
Kenneth Copeland
JESUS IS LORD!

CHAPTER 1

Take Your Place at the Father's Table

Oh, that men would give thanks to the LORD for His goodness, and for His wonderful works to the children of men! For He satisfies the longing soul, and fills the hungry soul with goodness.

Psalm 107:8-9

I've only heard it once.

In all my years of traveling and talking with Christians all over the world, only one person has ever said these words to me. "Dennis, I wouldn't change one thing about my life."

The statement carried no sense of complacency. No careless surrender to the status quo. Instead, it sparkled with contentment, bubbling up like a spring from a man who was living life the way it's meant to be lived.

Such springs are all too rare these days. People everywhere are parched. Thirsty for something more. Hungry for fulfillment they can't seem to find.

Most of us try, though. You have to give us credit for that. We gnaw away at life like a dog at a bone—with determination, gusto, and frequently with frustration. Working it from every angle, we labor to extract from our existence the satisfaction we crave. Yet, more often than not, we still feel like we're lacking something. Stomach growling, we always want more.

It's not a new phenomenon. It can't be blamed on Generation X, Y, or Z. It wasn't introduced by today's consumer culture. By cashiers at drive-through windows saying, "Would you like to supersize that?" Or by The Shopping Network. No, the dilemma of perpetual dissatisfaction has been around as long as people can remember. A few decades ago, it even caught the attention of the press. Hoping to shed some light on the situation, a news magazine surveyed thousands of Americans to find out just how much money they needed to be satisfied. "What would it take for you to live the American dream?" they were asked.

After averaging the answers, the magazine reported these results: People making $25,000 a year thought $54,000 would be enough. Those making $100,000 said $192,000 would satisfy them. And so on. Eventually, John D. Rockefeller, one of the richest men in the world at the time, weighed in on the issue. When asked how much money it takes to be truly rich, he gave a classic, unforgettable answer. "Just a little more," he said.

Marketing experts make millions by exploiting that mentality. They start by targeting toddlers with toy-laden cereal boxes. Stacking them knee-high on grocery store shelves where little eyes can see and little hands can reach, they provoke the familiar cry. *Mommy, I want it!*

So it begins...and so it continues. From childhood, to adolescence, to adulthood, to the grave. Always wanting more. Never having enough.

As Christians, we're not shocked when we see unbelievers trapped in such a cycle. Why shouldn't they be? The only system they know enshrines materialism as a god. But things should be different in the church, don't you think? Surely, we believers shouldn't be running here and there, seeking the same stuff everybody else does. Surely, we don't have to be driven by the same insatiable disease. Yet all too often we are.

Christians by the church-loads live in continual frustration because they don't have the cash to dress, drive, or vacation in the same kind of luxury their friends do. They mortgage themselves into misery, buying their way into upscale neighborhoods. Then they're eaten up with embarrassment because they don't have as much stuff as everybody else on the block.

What's up with that?

My answer may surprise you. Unlike some, I don't think the problem lies with our affluent society. I don't believe that Christians have simply been seduced by a covetous culture. Nor do I believe we can rediscover the secret of contentment by adopting a more austere lifestyle. I don't buy the idea that we can become less materialistic and more spiritually satisfied by wearing cheaper clothes, driving cheaper cars, and vacationing in tents in the backyard.

In other words, I'm not anti-stuff. I'm actually in favor of it. I like it. I like nice cars and homes. I *really* like nice motorcycles. And I don't mind saying so because I don't believe those things are the problem.

The problem is we've fallen for a lie. We've gone after stuff (in the form of things, money, status, success, et cetera) like a dog goes after a bone because we've swallowed the same deception the dog does. We've believed that such bones could satisfy our inner hunger. People want stuff like dogs want bones. That's what we've thought. But here's the hitch. Dogs don't really want bones. Dogs want meat. They've settled for bones.

So have we. In our quest to live an abundant life, we've settled for scraps. We've chased, chewed on, and coveted things that—although there's nothing wrong with them—were never meant to fulfill the hunger in our heart. We've fed on crumbs and stayed famished. Yet, all the while, our heavenly Father has a banquet table prepared for us. It's piled high with enough soul-satisfying goodness to take us from here to eternity. And there's a chair with our name on it. Sitting empty.

The solution to the problem seems so obvious it's a wonder so many Christians miss it. But multitudes do.

Maybe that's because they've been taught by well-meaning ministers that God's feast is in heaven and they can't enjoy it until they get there. Which would be fine if folks were planning to die or be raptured right away but most of them aren't. I've noticed when I minister that if I ask who's looking forward to heaven, hands fly up all over the congregation. People smile and cheer and wave. But when I ask if they want to go right now, the hands drop and the place goes silent. It seems that as hungry as believers might be for a satisfying life, if they have to pass through the pearly gates to get it, they'd rather wait and deal with their dissatisfaction some other way.

So that's what we do. We try to put the kibosh on our carnality by feeling guilty about it. We cut up our credit cards. Cancel our subscriptions to *Consumer's Guide*. Deprive ourselves of unnecessary indulgences and strive to be content with less. But those tactics by themselves don't work. We can't cure ourselves of materialism by cutting down on the amount of stuff in our lives any more than we could stop a starving man from eating out of a dumpster by putting him on a diet.

What we need to do is find our way to our Father's table. Not a table reserved for the next life that can only be reached by way of heaven, but a table available to us now. Psalm 23 describes it as a table *prepared for us in the presence of our enemies.*[1] Clearly, our enemies (which include the devil and everybody who's working for him) aren't waiting for us in heaven. They're doing their dirty work on earth which means the Psalm 23 buffet can be enjoyed right here.

---

[1] Psalm 23:5 KJV

Even so, some people hesitate to pull up a chair. They're afraid that what God is cooking up for them could be even less satisfying than the crumbs they've been eating. They remember the times they've messed up and suspect that their plate might be covered with cabbage and cod liver oil—a lifetime of hard lessons served up by a frowning God who considers such fare their just desserts.

People get that idea because it's the picture painted of God by every false religion in the world. It's the picture of an angry God who is generally unhappy and must be appeased. A God who is displeased with people most of the time. Somehow that pagan concept has crept into the church. It's convinced a great number of Christians that God is—at the very least—irritated with them. They believe that He's saved them and given them hope for the hereafter, and they're grateful for it. But they're not expecting Him to do much for them between now and then.

As a result, the majority of Christians need the same reassurance needed by people who are practically strangers to the Scriptures. First, they need to know that God is a good God. That He loves them and wants to do good things for them. In other words, they need to know that God wants to be, not their judge or their punisher, but their Papa.

Once we receive Jesus as Lord, God is our Papa, you know. According to the Bible, that's what our spirit calls Him. "For ye have not received the spirit of bondage again to fear; but ye have received the Spirit of adoption, whereby we cry, Abba, Father" (Romans 8:15 KJV). The Greek word *Abba* means Daddy, or Papa. I know something about that word not because I'm a Greek scholar but because I'm a grandfather and that's what my grandchildren call me. Nothing lights me up any more than being their Papa. I love it. In my grandchildren's eyes, Papa can do anything. He's master of the universe. He's a king (at least in his own mind) who delights in them and wants to bless them in every conceivable way.

Why am I like that? Why do we as parents and grand-parents have such a deep-rooted desire to drench our children and grandchildren with goodness? Because we're made in God's image. We're created in the likeness of our heavenly Papa, and that's how He is. A Father who *daily loads us with benefits,*[2] He is a good God!

Here's the second thing I've found that believers everywhere need to know: God wants to be good to us not just in the sweet by and by, but right here and now. If we put our faith in Him, good things can start happening in our lives today. Jesus left no doubt about it. He summed up His whole mission on earth—His reason for dying on the cross and bearing mankind's sins—by saying: "My purpose is to give them a rich and satisfying life."[3]

A rich and satisfying life. It's what we've all been hungry for; it's what Jesus came to give; and it's what the Bible promises us again and again in verses like these:

- "My people shall be satisfied with My goodness, says the Lord" (Jeremiah 31:14).

[2] Psalm 68:19 NKJV
[3] John 10:10

- "He satisfies the longing soul, and fills the hungry soul with goodness" (Psalm 107:9).

- "Therefore the children of men put their trust under the shadow of Your wings. They are abundantly satisfied with the fullness of Your house, and You give them drink from the river of Your pleasures" (Psalm 36:7-8).

- "With long life I will satisfy him, and show him my salvation" (Psalm 91:16).

More than Just Longevity

Look again at that last verse. It's long been one of my personal favorites, but I didn't always see the full meaning of it. I used to assume that when God said He'd satisfy us with long life and show us His salvation, He was just promising us a lot of years on this planet. Eventually, however, it dawned on me He had much more in mind.

After all, long life doesn't always equal satisfaction. It's possible to live long and be miserable, sick, and broke. It's possible to be ancient and unhappy. (Most of us have relatives who've proven it.) So when God says He'll satisfy us with long life, He's promising more than longevity. He's promising many years of a life worth living. He's describing a life that fulfills our desires, exceeds our expectations, and leaves us crowing with contentment.

If you doubt it, look up the Hebrew word for *salvation*. You'll find it doesn't just refer to getting us to heaven and saving us from hell. It's defined as *deliverance from every kind of evil—both temporal and eternal.* It includes victory, prosperity, security, and freedom from distress. God's salvation is richer than anything we've imagined and, according to the Bible, He not only wants to show it *to* us, He wants to show it *through* us. He wants to flood our lives with His blessing and goodness so that He "can always point to us as examples of the incredible wealth of his favor and kindness toward us, as shown in all he has done for us through Christ Jesus."[4]

Can you wrap your mind around this? God intends for our lives to be so satisfying in every way, so brimming with His bounty, that we become living illustrations of His favor and kindness. He plans for us, as believers, to be like billboards advertising His love and blessings. He wants a lost world to look at what He's done for us and say, "I want it!"

That's why crumbs don't satisfy us. God didn't design us to live on such a low level. He didn't create us to be mediocre or average. It's not in our divine DNA.

We're ordained by God to be spectacular. As Christians, we're part of His worldwide agenda to demonstrate the glory, greatness, and goodness of Jesus. We're meant to be on display as showpieces of God's grace. We're made for victory, to stand in the authority of Jesus and conquer everything the kingdom of darkness throws at us. As 1 Peter 2:9 says, we're *a chosen race, a royal priesthood, a dedicated nation, [God's] own purchased, special people,* called to *set forth the wonderful deeds and display the*

---

[4] Ephesians 2:7

virtues and perfections of Him Who called us out of darkness into His marvelous light.[5]

Talk about a satisfying life! What could be better than a lifetime spent revealing the blessings of God given to mankind through the Lord Jesus Christ?

Nothing! That's as good as it gets. And it's what we're called by God to do.

We all do it in different ways because God has a unique assignment for each one of us. Mine involves getting on an airplane every week and going somewhere to proclaim the gospel. Somebody else's might involve selling cars or practicing law or landscaping lawns. The details of God's plan for us as individuals differ. But the purpose stays the same. We're here to show off the goodness and salvation of God. That's our divine assignment. When we do it, our dissatisfaction disappears. Our stomach stops growling because we're not settling for bones anymore. We've gotten hold of the real thing.

Jesus said it this way, "My food is to do the will of Him who sent Me, and to finish His work" (John 4:35).

Now that's what I call a meal.

Spiritual Fulfillment with a Generous Side of Stuff

Although the kind of meal our Father offers can't be found scrounging around on the floor of materialism, make no mistake, material things are included in it. God specifically says so. He tells us clearly in the Scriptures

---

[5] The Amplified Bible

that in addition to rich spiritual fare—like love, peace, joy, and righteousness—He's spread His table with lots of natural stuff. In Matthew 6:24-33, for instance, Jesus promised God will feed us as plentifully as He feeds the birds. (Most of them eat their weight in food every day, but I don't recommend following their example.) He'll dress us as extravagantly as Solomon (the richest man in history) and as fashionably as the lilies (they get a new wardrobe every year).

That's why I'm not anti-stuff. God wants us to have it. He "gives us richly all things to enjoy"[6] not only because He loves us, but also because we need those material blessings to complete our assignment. It's tough to bless others and reveal to the world how truly good our heavenly Father is when we have holes in our shoes and nothing in our pockets. It's hard to sell sinners on a seemingly stingy God. They have enough stinginess in their lives already.

Unbelievers need to see some Christians who enjoy life. They need to see believers who are convincing billboards for every aspect of the abundant life—spirit, soul, and body. That's what people who don't yet know the Lord are looking for. They're not hungry for long-faced religious piety. They don't want a carefully crafted sermon with three points and a poem. They want LIFE at its best—the kind of life that will make them smile, meet their needs, and satisfy the gnawing in the pit of their souls. They want what I wanted back in 1971. I'd just gotten born again back then. Fresh out of a dope-smoking, sin-loving, hippie lifestyle, I didn't have much spiritual depth. I definitely wasn't the brightest candle in God's window.

---

[6] 1 Timothy 6:17

But like any baby—spiritual or otherwise—I was smart enough to know I was hungry.

So I went to church.

With no one to guide me, no mentors to help, I just chose the closest church I could find. It looked good on the outside but on Sunday morning I went in and found out that looks don't always tell the whole story. Slipping onto the back row and taking a seat, I wondered if I'd misread the sign in front. Was this a church or a museum? The place seemed to be filled with fossils. I'm not saying the people there were old, just that they showed no detectible signs of spiritual life.

Rather than reading from the Bible, the minister quoted newspaper articles and offered his opinions. His points may have been interesting (I can't remember for sure) but they lacked the divine life I was hungering for.

Jesus said, "The words that I speak to you are spirit, and they are life."[7] Without the Word, there's no life. Somehow, even as a spiritual infant, I understood that. So I left the First Church of Fossils and never went back.

Thank God, shortly thereafter I did find a church that taught the Word. And I'll be bold enough to tell you, if you want a satisfied life, that's one of the first things you should do. But going to church, in itself, isn't enough. Church services once or twice a week aren't meant to be the sum total of our spiritual experience. They can help us. They can get us headed in the right direction. They can encourage and build us up. But to experience the

---

[7] John 6:63

kind of satisfaction described in Psalm 91:16, we must do more than go to church. We must follow the example of the man described in verse 1 of that Psalm and dwell *in the secret place of the Most High.*

What is the secret place?

To me, it's the place of private fellowship with God. A place of ongoing dialogue and vital relationship where we listen to what He has to say to us and respond with love and obedience. It's not a place we just visit now and then, not a place we drop by every once in a while. It's our home, the place in our heart that we return to again and again; and because God is never boring, it's the most thrilling place on earth.

People who just dabble with Christianity know little about the secret place. Those who read God's Word only on occasion and pray only when they're in trouble miss out on its blessings. But those who pick up and move there discover the kind of rich and satisfying life everybody wants. They enjoy the benefits that, according to Psalm 91:1, are available only to those who make "*the shadow of the Almighty*" their permanent address.

Living in a shadow doesn't sound like a big deal to us today but back when David penned Psalm 91, it was major. In his day, riding camel-back under the scorching sun, you couldn't just roll up the windows and crank up the air conditioning. When the sand sizzled and the temperature soared, you couldn't beat the heat by adjusting the thermostat. You needed some shade.

On the hottest of days that shade could save your life. Whoever invented the umbrella figured that out. The term *umbra* is Latin for *shade*. Umbrellas got their start protecting people from the sun, not the rain. Some overheated soul, tired of being sunburned, came up with them so that people could carry their own personal shade everywhere they went.

I'm sure the first umbrella was a marvelous thing and everybody rejoiced over it. But it was nothing compared to the umbrella God offers us. His shadow protects us 24/7 from the dangers of this world where, despite our modern conveniences and controls, we have no other real security. The shade of His supernatural favor keeps us cool no matter how hot things get. We never have to sweat it when we're dwelling in the secret place with our loving Father and Almighty God.

Why, then, doesn't everybody live there?

They would if it was as easy as buying an umbrella and strolling down the street. But it's not. Living in the secret place requires an internal revolution. It requires us to exchange the unsatisfactory materialistic system devised by the world for one that's supernaturally superior. It requires us to actively, purposely dethrone the old ways of thinking that have dominated our lives and replace them with the thoughts and ways of God.

I won't kid you, that kind of revolution takes work. It doesn't happen by accident, falling on us like acorns off a tree while we sit around hoping something changes. It doesn't drop in our lap while we're waiting for God to show up and fix the mess in our lives.

The scriptural truth is, God has already showed up. He's already promised and provided more than we can ask or think. He's sent Jesus, prepared a table with everything we need to live rich and satisfying lives, and even reserved a seat with our name on it.

We're not waiting for God anymore. He's waiting for us.

Supper's ready. Come on, let's eat.

Don't Sweat the Small Stuff (or the Big Stuff Either)

Live carefree before God; he is most careful with you.

1 Peter 5:7 The Message

I once spent an entire afternoon aggravated over a dispute about spotted owls. I didn't mean to, of course. I got involved with the issue by accident one day while driving down the road listening to the news on the radio.

It seems odd now, looking back, that such a silly thing could bother me. You'd think the newscaster's negative descriptions of world affairs and the economy would have created more concern. But for whatever reason, I stayed sunny until the subject of spotted owls came up. Then, I clouded over. Turning up the volume, I learned with mounting irritation about the battle between the owl-protectors and the loggers whose livelihood purportedly poses a threat to the owl's survival. And the more I heard, the more annoyed I became.

To be honest, I've never actually seen a spotted owl. Nor can I count a single lumberjack among my close circle of friends. But my lack of personal involvement in the situation didn't stop me from getting irritated about it. Suddenly, out of the airwaves, a cause had been thrust upon me. The peace I'd enjoyed moments before dissolved. I gripped the steering wheel tighter and shook my head.

What a ludicrous situation! I thought. *What a travesty! How can people be so dense?!*

I'm not telling which side of the issue I took. Let's just say that, erupting in exasperation, I cried out (to no one, since I was alone in the car) either, "Recycle wood! Save the owls!" or "Let the owls relocate! Cut the lumber!" Feel free to pick the phrase you find least offensive.

My worry over the owl problem didn't last long, you'll be glad to hear. I quickly let it go. After all, I know full well that the Word of God says, "Don't worry about anything; instead, pray about everything."[8] And though I didn't pray for the owls (or the loggers either for that matter) by the time I got where I was going that afternoon, I wasn't worried about them anymore. Which was good. Because it's impossible to worry and live a satisfied life at the same time. It's impossible to experience the kind of rich, abundant life that Jesus offers when your stomach churns with anxiety and your thoughts are crowded with cares. That's why the Bible so often gives us commands like this:

---

[8] Philippians 4:6 NLT

- "Do not fret" (Psalm 37:7).

- "Do not fear" (Luke 12:32).

- "Be anxious for nothing" (Philippians 4:6).

- "Give all your worries and cares to God, for he cares about what happens to you" (1 Peter 5:7 NLT).

Keeping those commands would be easy if spotted owls were our only problem. But they're not. These days, especially, much more serious issues concern us. Personally. Nationally. Globally. Economically. Trouble threatens on every side. Options for worrying abound.

For high-level worriers, these are glorious times. If we choose, we can worry about any number of things. I know people who've committed themselves to it and become absolutely world-class worriers. Because they think worrying is the responsible thing to do, they even worry about people who don't have sense enough to worry. If they're compassionate, they may even put in some extra worry time on other folks' behalf to help them along.

I don't mean to mock those people. I can understand why they're worried. This world is a dangerous place. Bad things happen. They really do. Even the Bible talks about it. Right there in Psalm 91 where God promises us a satisfied life, He refers to things like terror, pestilence, and destruction. Those things are out there! To pretend otherwise isn't faith, it's foolishness.

What's the solution, then? How can we be realistic and still remain worry free?

Thank heaven, Psalm 91 tells us. It says:

He who dwells in the secret place of the Most High Shall abide under the shadow of the Almighty. I will say of the LORD, 'He is my refuge and my fortress; My God, in Him I will trust.' Surely He shall deliver you from the snare of the fowler and from the perilous pestilence. He shall cover you with His feathers, and under His wings you shall take refuge (verses 1-4).

According to those verses, the critics who call Christianity a crutch or an escape are right. That's exactly what it is. It's a hiding place, a refuge from the hazards that surround us and I, for one, am glad. It's wonderful to have a refuge in stormy times like these. A refuge, by definition, provides shelter or protection from danger and trouble. It's a place of safety. It's something or Someone we can turn to for aid or relief.

Everybody likes to have a good place to hide when life gets rough. Don't give me that stuff about keeping a stiff upper lip and taking trouble on the chin. Nobody in their right mind does that. In the middle of a battlefield when the enemy is firing, nobody says, "I think I'll just stand here and take a bullet in the chest." Are you kidding? Everybody looks for cover in a war zone. Everybody wants a fox hole, a refuge, or a fortress when the bombs are dropping and the bullets are flying.

As believers, we have that kind of protection available to us all the time. Through our relationship with God, we not only have somebody to talk to when difficulties arise, someone who cares about our problems, we have Someone with the power and the commitment to do something about them. Almighty God has given us His Word that

"...as the mountains surround and protect Jerusalem, so the LORD surrounds and protects his people, both now and forever."[9] He's promised us that "the God-begotten are also the God-protected. The Evil One can't lay a hand on them."[10] So no matter what's happening around us, we can look to Him and say, "You are my hiding place; You shall preserve me from trouble; You shall surround me with songs of deliverance."[11]

"But Dennis, if that's true, why don't we see more evidence of God's protection in our lives? Why do Christians so often suffer the same calamities experienced by everybody else?"

Because we don't always activate His power the way Psalm 91 tells us to. We don't boldly and consistently declare by faith, "The Lord is my refuge and fortress! He is my God in whom I trust. Surely He will deliver me!"

Instead, we just try to have a positive mental attitude. We endeavor inwardly to trust the Lord, but when the pressure hits and things really start to look bad, we spout the same stuff unbelievers do. If we sneeze, we're likely to say, "Oh, no! I must be coming down with that bird flu! It never fails. If anything is going around, I always get it. So do my kids. We'll be sick for weeks, sure as can be."

May I make a suggestion? When you're tempted to make those kinds of statements, please, for your own sake—and I say this with great love—*Do yourself a favor! Shut your mouth!*

---

[9] Psalm 125:2 NLT
[10] 1 John 5:18 The Message
[11] Psalm 32:7

What we say is powerful. It brings alignment into our life. Our words either put us in agreement with God or with the devil. When symptoms of sickness come on us, we ought to say things like, "I'm not taking the flu of any kind. I don't care whether it came from a bird or a swine or a city called Hong Kong, I don't have to put up with it because I've been inoculated. I've been immunized, not by some FDA approved vaccine, but by the Word and power of Almighty God."

"I'd feel silly saying something like that," you might say. "I'm just not that sure of myself!"

You don't have to be sure of yourself. You just have to be sure of your God. You just have to believe that if you dwell in the secret place and confess Him as your Deliverer, He will do for you exactly what the Bible says:

"He shall cover you with His feathers, and under His wings you shall take refuge; His truth shall be your shield and buckler. You shall not be afraid of the terror by night, nor of the arrow that flies by day, nor of the pestilence that walks in darkness, nor of the destruction that lays waste at noonday. A thousand may fall at your side, and ten thousand at your right hand; but it shall not come near you. Because you have made the LORD, who is my refuge, even the Most High, your dwelling place, no evil shall befall you, nor shall any plague come near your dwelling; for He shall give His angels charge over you, to keep you in all your ways. In their hands they shall bear you up, lest you dash your foot against a stone" (Psalm 91:4-7,9-12).

Snatched Out of the Snare

Some time ago, I was studying the protection promised in Psalm 91 and I noticed that the word *deliver* is repeated there three times. Verses 3, 14, and 15 all declare that God will deliver us. Sometimes the Bible uses such repetition simply for emphasis, but after doing some research I discovered that's not what's happening here. In this case, the English word *deliver* is translated from three different and distinct Hebrew words, indicating that God has supplied a three-way security system so that we can live in this world with complete peace of mind.

We find the first aspect of the security system in verse 3 where God promises to deliver us from the snare of the fowler. A snare is a trap and it's a bad place to be. Have you ever seen a little animal caught in a net, a cage, or a spring-loaded trap set by a hunter? No matter how frantically the poor creature struggles, it can't get free. It's completely helpless.

We all know what that's like because we've been there. We've all gotten caught in the devil's snares. A diabolical hunter out to destroy us, the devil is the enemy of our souls. He strategizes against us, designing pitfalls for our defeat. Sometimes he uses circumstances, other people, or the forces of this fallen world to ensnare us in situations we had no part in creating. Other times he traps us by exploiting our own fleshly weaknesses, or by using the issues of life to distract us and get our focus off God and His Word.

31

Embarrassing as it is to admit, there are even times when we stumble into snares all by ourselves, without any help from the devil at all. Human beings can sometimes be so skilled at screwing things up that the devil can hardly keep up with us. He has to be notified so that he can take credit.

Regardless of how we end up there, once we're in a snare, we can't get free by ourselves. Whether we're trapped by fear, or offense, a broken relationship, pornography, debt, or failure in some area of life (the list could go on and on) we can't find our own way out. We need somebody to come help us, to pull us out of whatever pit we've fallen into.

According to the Hebrew word used in Psalm 91:3, that's exactly what God does. He delivers us by snatching us up out of trouble. He grabs us and yanks us out of the impossible situation we're entangled in.

"Will He do that for me even if the situation is my own dumb fault?" somebody might ask. "Even if I goofed things up all on my own?"

Yes, He will. He's not mad at you. You haven't upset Him so much that you've turned Him off from wanting to deliver you. You can't turn Him off. He's in love with you and He's always on your side. So if you'll look in the right direction, if you'll get your eyes on Him and put faith in His Word, He'll give you all the help you need.

There's no snare too big for God to handle. No trap He can't spring. Even when all the evidence indicates that the situation you're facing is hopeless, He can turn it around. The Bible confirms it again and again. Take the apostle Paul, for example. God repeatedly delivered him from every kind of snare you can imagine.

Before he became a Christian, he was duped by the devil into persecuting the early church. He traveled around dragging believers out of their homes and putting them in prison. Fully convinced that he was doing God a favor, Paul was caught in a trap so strong and subtle that he had no idea he was in it! He wasn't even looking for a way out. Yet—most likely because of the prayers of the early church—Jesus appeared to Paul on the road to Damascus and snatched him out of that trap.

Once he got born again, Paul found himself in snares that weren't his fault at all. They were set-ups of the devil meant to keep him from preaching the gospel. One of those set-ups turned out to be so dangerous that it appeared Paul and his ministry companions would never make it through alive. It seemed to them there was no way out. In his letter to the Corinthians, Paul described it this way:

> *"For we do not want you to be uniformed, brethren, about the affliction and oppressing distress which befell us in [the province of] Asia, how we were so utterly and unbearably weighed down and crushed that we despaired even of life [itself]. Indeed, we felt within ourselves that we had received the [very] sentence of death..." (2 Corinthians 1:8-9 AMP).*

Do you believe that God can deliver you from a problem so massive that it's a veritable death sentence? Paul and his friends did! They put their faith in "God who raises the dead,"[12] and He responded just like Psalm 91 said He would. As Paul said, "[He] *delivered* us from so great a death, and *does deliver* us; in whom we trust that He *will still deliver* us."[13] Notice that Paul, much like the psalmist, used the word deliver three times in that verse to emphasize the fact that God's deliverance covers us in every situation. It covers our past, present, and future.

Don't you love it? No matter how deep a hole the devil digs for us, God can reach down and pull us out! He can spring any trap Satan comes up with any place, any time! So say it by faith right now, "God is my refuge and fortress. I trust Him to rescue me, save me, and snatch me out of every snare. He's my God. He has delivered me, He does deliver me, and He will deliver me!"

Into Avoidance

It's hard to imagine that anybody—even God—could top the snare-snatching kind of deliverance. I mean, really. What could be better?

How about this: never getting into the snare in the first place.

According to Psalm 91, it's possible. God will help us do it.

In verse 14, He says of the secret place dweller that "Because he has set his love upon Me, therefore I will deliver him; I will set him on high, because he has known My name." In this instance, the Hebrew word translated

---

[12] 2 Corinthians 1:9
[13] Verse 10, emphasis mine.

deliver doesn't refer to being yanked out of trouble we've already gotten into; it conveys the idea of being lifted and carried away to safety so that we avoid trouble completely. I'm excited by that concept. When it comes to trouble, I'm totally into avoidance and I'm thrilled to know that it's available to us if we'll follow the guidance system God has put inside us.

When we're tuned into that guidance system (a.k.a. the leading of the Holy Spirit) God can warn us ahead of time about the traps the devil has set up. He can give us a little nudge and lead us to take another route home from work, for instance, so we avoid a traffic accident without even realizing it.

That's the way this kind of deliverance works. It lifts you over snares or steers you around them. Sometimes you never know they were there. Other times you see, looking back, that one simple decision kept you from falling into a major pit. But you have to follow the nudge! You have to let the Holy Spirit lead you. That's why dwelling in the secret place and spending time with God every day in His Word is so vital. It keeps your thinking aligned with God's. It keeps your heart keen to the promptings of His Spirit so you don't think it's your imagination when you're about to make a business decision and you sense the Spirit saying to you, *Don't make this deal. Don't go into partnership with that person.*

Just think about how many problems such warnings could spare you! Think how much turmoil you could avoid by obeying the Holy Spirit and zipping your lips at exactly the right time. If you're having an animated discussion with your spouse and the Lord says to you,

Stop! Don't finish that sentence! just hearing and heeding His warning could save you a night on the couch, or even a wrecked marriage.

I see people all the time who could have enjoyed that kind of deliverance. But they missed out on it because they didn't put God first in their lives. They didn't fix their heart on Him in advance, before trouble came. So they messed up their life, created havoc in their family, went broke, got head-over-heels in debt, and then had to say, "Uh, God, could You help me out?"

He does help folks in such situations, of course, because He's good and He loves them. But their lives could have been much more satisfying if they'd called out to Him in advance. He could have lifted them up over all that junk. He could have helped them walk above it in a place of safety so that they never had to go through it.

Armed and Dangerous

I'm not suggesting we can live in such a way that we avoid difficulties completely. Jesus told us, "In this world you will have trouble,"[14] and sometimes that trouble comes straight at us. It bears down on us like an 18-wheeler in a tunnel and avoidance is not an option. What do we do when that happens?

We reach for the third kind of deliverance. We follow the example of the man in Psalm 91:15 about whom God says, "He shall call upon Me, and I will answer him; I will be with him in trouble; I will deliver him and honor

---

[14] John 16:33 NIV

him." The Hebrew word for deliverance used there is a dramatic departure from the other two words. This one refers to being equipped for battle. By choosing this word, God is saying, "You're not going around this fight. You're going through it and you're going to win it because I've equipped you. I've given you every weapon you need. I've provided you with all the strength and resources necessary to crush any enemy that comes against you. You are armed to the max. You have what it takes to confront this trouble and blow it out of your life."

I know what you may be thinking. You're wondering if that's really true in your case. But there's no need for you to wonder. I can tell you on the authority of God's Word, if you're a born again child of Almighty God, you have the goods. You've got what it takes to overcome anything the devil throws at you.

You have the Spirit of God dwelling inside you, and the Bible says that "He who is in you is greater than he who is in the world."[15]

You have "the sword of the Spirit, which is the word of God."[16]

You have the Name of Jesus which has authority over "every name that is named, not only in this age but also in that which is to come."[17]

You have the abundance of God's grace which is nothing less than His supernatural empowerment to triumph in every situation. God has said to you as He said to Paul,

[15] 1 John 4:4
[16] Ephesians 6:17
[17] Ephesians 1:21

"My grace is sufficient for you, for My strength is made perfect in weakness."[18]

You have the capacity to speak in a heavenly language and pray perfect prayers by the Holy Spirit who "makes intercession for the saints according to the will of God."[19]

You have the power to "resist the devil and he will flee from you."[20]

You have the ability to "take up the whole armor of God, that you may be able to withstand in the evil day... having girded your waist with truth, having put on the breastplate of righteousness, and having shod your feet with the preparation of the gospel of peace; above all, taking the shield of faith with which you will be able to quench all the fiery darts of the wicked one."[21]

You even have unseen angelic help working with you, "ministering spirits sent forth to minister"[22] for you as an heir of salvation.

All the demons in hell and Satan himself are help-less in the face of all the equipment you've been given. When they attack you, they're counting on the fact that you won't use it. I hate to say it, but most believers don't. That's why statistically Christians in general aren't experiencing any more success than non-Christians. Their divorce rate is about the same; they have the same kinds of financial failures and emotional problems; which

---

[18] 2 Corinthians 12:9
[19] Romans 8:27
[20] James 4:7
[21] Ephesians 6:13-16
[22] Hebrews 1:14

means that for the most part Christians aren't picking up their weapons. They go to church, hear a sermon, feel a little better, and then go home. They aren't taking the truths of their victory in Jesus and applying them to their everyday lives.

If they were, we'd hear a lot more stories like the one I saw on the news a couple of years ago. It featured a woman who knew how to use her God-given trouble-conquering equipment. The owner of a store in a city not far from where I live, she was waiting on a customer one day when a hooded gunman walked in, pointed a 45-caliber pistol in her face, and demanded money.

If the surveillance camera hadn't caught it all on video, what happened next would be hard to believe. The shop owner didn't bat an eye. She didn't show a trace of fear. Instead, she stuck her finger in the gunman's face and said, "You get out of here, in the Name of Jesus!"

For a few seconds, everybody froze. The gunman stood holding his gun. The shop owner stood pointing her finger. The customer stood bug-eyed and bewildered muttering, "Oh, my God!"

Both the gunman and the customer spent that sliver of time wondering which one was going to win: the gun in the robber's hand, or the finger in the Name of Jesus. The shop owner settled the question. Wagging her finger with bewildering ferocity, she made her demand again. "I said, get out of here, in Jesus' Name!"

Sure enough, the gunman turned around and bolted out of the store just like he came in, empty handed. Can't you just see him scratching his head, trying to figure out what happened? *How come I have a gun and I'm running from a lady armed with nothing but a finger?* he must have wondered.

Or, then again, maybe that's not what he was thinking at all. Maybe he was wondering how all those huge security guards dressed in white suddenly appeared out of nowhere. Maybe God opened his eyes like He opened the eyes of Elisha's servant and let him see into the realm of the spirit. If you've read the story in the Old Testament, you probably remember that Elisha was facing far more than a single gunman with a pistol. He was surrounded by horses, chariots, and a Syrian army—and they were all on a mission to kill him. When his servant saw them, he panicked and cried out, "Alas, my master! What shall we do?"

Elisha, however, wasn't worried at all. He knew that God had equipped him with more than enough supernatural firepower to see him through. So he answered, "Do not fear, for those who are with us are more than those who are with them."

The Bible doesn't say so, but I imagine at that point the servant did some quick counting. He looked at himself and at Elisha and said, "One...two." Then he looked at the thousands of Syrian soldiers. *Hmmm.* He looked back at himself and Elisha. "One...two." Just when the servant was about to decide that the prophet of God had lost his mind, Elisha prayed, and said, "LORD...open his eyes that he may see."

"Then the LORD opened the eyes of the young man, and he saw. And behold, the mountain was full of horses and chariots of fire all around Elisha."[23] God's angelic army totally trumped Syria's, so Elisha won the battle hands down. He took his enemies captive (yes, all of them) and "the bands of Syrian raiders came no more into the land of Israel."[24]

That's how trouble turns out when we understand and use the equipment of God.

So what's to worry about? Why should we waste a moment fretting over anything? God has it all covered (spotted owls and lumberjacks notwithstanding). He hasn't left us to fend for ourselves in these dangerous days. He hasn't left us on our own. His three-fold deliverance is always there for us.

If we fall into a snare, God will snatch us out of it. If we tune into His guidance system, He will lift us above trouble and carry us to a place of safety. If doing battle is the only option, He's equipped us to win every time.

In all these things, we are more than conquerors through Him who loves us. So, don't sweat the small stuff...or the big stuff...or the stuff in between. Just say of the Lord, "He is my refuge and my fortress; my God, in Him will I trust." Then relax, and enjoy a safe and satisfying life.

---

[23] 2 Kings 6:16-17
[24] Verse 23

Get on the Right Road

And do not [for a moment] be frightened or intimidated in anything by your opponents and adversaries, for such [constancy and fearlessness] will be a clear sign (proof and seal) to them of [their impending] destruction, but [a sure token and evidence] of your deliverance and salvation, and that from God.

Philippians 1:28 AMP

Dreams of divine destiny rarely include a trip to the dentist.

None of us, when asked to imagine God's plan for our life, visualize ourselves with a white paper bib dangling from our neck, mouth open wider than our Creator ever intended, with the muffled moan of drilling in our ears. I daresay there's not a soul on earth who ever considered a root canal to be an essential part of a satisfied life.

As far as I'm concerned, that's just as it should be. After all, the Bible doesn't say one thing about dental work.

There are scriptures that apply to it, of course. Some of those I've already mentioned, such as *In the world ye shall have tribulation but be of good cheer... Be anxious for nothing...*and *Fear not,* come to mind. Those exhortations can be helpful when a receptionist chirps with deceptive glee, "The dentist will see you now!" So it's good to remember them at such times.

Usually, however, it's not a life or death matter. Neither dental appointments nor what we think about them tend to be any big deal in the overall scheme of things. At least, that's what I always assumed until I read an article from a London newspaper a few years ago. It recounted the story of a woman whose negative thoughts about going to the dentist actually changed the course of her future.

The thoughts began with a trauma she experienced early in life. As a little girl, she'd accompanied her mother to a dentist appointment. While her mother sat having teeth cleaned and cavities filled, under the careful hands of the dentist and the watchful eyes of her daughter, tragedy struck. The mother suffered a massive heart attack and died instantly.

In the dentist's chair.

Her death had nothing to do with the dental procedures. (A fact which will comfort you, I'm sure, if you happen to have an upcoming appointment.) But in the little girl's mind, it did. Convinced that what happened to her mother would happen to her, she decided to avoid dental offices...forever.

As the years passed and the little girl grew up, instead of outgrowing her fear, the fear grew along with her, forcing her to forgo the oral care she desperately needed. By the time she reached her mid-thirties, her teeth were in serious trouble. The throbbing could no longer be ignored. Dental work had to be done, so she concocted a plan to survive it. She asked her physician to go with her to the dentist's office. Surely, she reasoned, with a bonafide medical doctor by her side to attend to her if anything happened, she'd make it through alive.

As it turned out, she was wrong.

When the dentist began his work, her fears finished theirs. The condition in her own soul created the very circumstances she'd spent a lifetime avoiding. Years of thoughts entertained and words spoken converged and became her reality. Right there in the dentist's chair she was stricken with a heart attack just like her mother. It was so sudden and massive that her doctor was unable to help her.

The title of the article that recounted the story?

"Killed by Thirty Years of Thought."

With that headline, the journalist captured the absolute truth. This was no freak coincidence. It was no unexplainable twist of fate. It was a dramatic snapshot of a universal truth in operation—a truth that echoes throughout the Bible again and again:

- "As he thinks in his heart, so is he" (Proverbs 23:7).

- "What you have believed has happened" (Matthew 8:13 NLT).

- "According to your faith let it be to you" (Matthew 9:29).

Such scriptures, while sobering, aren't meant to inspire gloom. They don't doom us all to the kind of end experienced by the lady in London. On the contrary! They shine with a magnificent and empowering up side that, if she'd understood it, would have changed everything for her. They deliver to us the marvelous news that we have the capacity to use our thoughts to create our own future, that our destiny isn't imposed on us by forces beyond our control; it's something we choose.

Many Christians would be shocked by that revelation. They've been religiously taught that their destiny is solely in the hands of God. I don't know where we got such an idea. It's not scriptural and, to be honest, it doesn't even make good sense. Obviously, it wasn't God who frightened that young woman to death in the dentist's chair. Any clear thinking person must admit that He'd never come up with such a twisted plan.

He did, however, have a plan for her. I don't know what it was. But I'm sure He had one.

He has a plan for all of us. He has a predetermined picture of how blessed and free and fulfilled we can be. He has an awesome destiny, a *good and acceptable and perfect will,*[25] a delightfully divine destination that was prepared for us *before the foundation of the world.*[26]

Bumping Down Back Roads

Much as I hate to say it, however, most people miss their God-ordained destiny.

Multitudes of good Christians who love the Lord fail to walk in the freedom, fulfillment, and victory that belong to them as believers. They stop short of the long, abundant, satisfying life God meant for them to live. Like the woman in the article, they let some trauma or trifle hijack their thinking and get them off track. Mentally, they take a wrong turn, so instead of finding the road God meant for them to travel, they stumble onto another and wind up somewhere disappointing and unsatisfying. Someplace God never intended them to go.

Truth be told, we've all taken those kinds of detours at one time or another. Barreling down life's highway, we've all gotten distracted. Gesturing our indignation at an offensive fellow traveler or rubbernecking at somebody else's fender-bender, we've missed crucial road signs (like *Exit Here for God's Perfect Will)* and found ourselves bumping down some seemingly God-forsaken back road wondering where in the sam hill we are.

That doesn't mean, however, we have to spend our lives out in the middle of nowhere. A few missed opportunities aren't the end of the line. God always has more in store for us and, if we'll dare to believe it, He can get

[25] Romans 12:2
[26] Ephesians 1:4

47

us back on the right track no matter how far afield we've wandered.

I once got a fresh revelation of that reality as I was stepping on the platform to preach to a congregation of convicts in a Texas penitentiary. I had a message already prepared for the occasion but at the last minute, the Lord downloaded into my spirit an entirely different message. (I don't know why it happens that way. I spend hours studying the Word and asking God for direction. But, for some reason known only to Him, He often waits until the service is starting to say these things to me. I'm not complaining, just making an observation. But, getting back to the story...) Just as I was about to take the microphone, He prompted me to begin my message by saying, "It's very likely that a lot of you have missed some good opportunities. It's likely that you find yourself where you are today because you didn't make the best choices. You didn't do everything exactly right."

Uh...you think? Deep thoughts from Dennis for prison inmates.

Despite the obvious nature of those opening insights, what came next surprised even me. I informed the members of my literally captive audience that they had a lot in common with a man in the New Testament named James. The half brother of the Lord Jesus Christ, James was the universally revered saint who, after Jesus' death and resurrection, became a pillar of the early church and authored one of the New Testament Epistles. What could a congregation of convicted criminals possibly have in common with such a man?

"Like James, you are people who have missed some good opportunities," I said. "Just as he did, you've made some seriously wrong choices. I don't know what yours have been, but his worst one was this: he rejected the earthly ministry of Jesus."

It's not exactly a point I ever expected to use as the centerpiece for a sermon, but it's true nonetheless. James grew up in the same household with the Lord. He watched Him on a daily basis living as the Word made flesh. Yet, he (along with the rest of Jesus' family) refused throughout the three years of Jesus' ministry to believe He was the Messiah. So, while his brother traveled around working miracles, healing the sick, raising the dead, and teaching the Word of God, James stayed home and remained an unbeliever.

Talk about missed opportunities! When Jesus stepped out into ministry, James could have followed Him. He could have seen the paralytic, lowered down through the roof by four faithful friends, pick up his bed and walk. He could have watched Lazarus wobble, wrapped in grave clothes, out of the darkness of his tomb. He could have listened in wonder as Jesus preached the messages that would forever bless mankind.

But James missed it all. He chose to travel a different road. The wrong road.

I'm not saying that James was out carousing around like an outlaw during those years. He was probably living a good, respectable life. I imagine he was like a lot of folks today—staying busy, trying to be religious and say enough prayers, striving to be a basically good person.

But as anybody who's familiar with wrong roads has discovered, it doesn't matter how many good things you do while you're on them, they still won't get you to your destination.

Say for instance, you're in San Diego and you want to drive to Dallas. You can take Highway 15. You can drive that highway for the rest of your life. You can give generous tips to every waitress in every roadside restaurant. You can sit reverently behind the steering wheel and sing Kum-ba-ya until your tonsils fall out. You can check out all the rest stops (and you will because you'll need them) and leave them all cleaner than you found them. But you'll still never get to Dallas *because Highway 15 doesn't go there!*

It sounds absurd, I know, but people actually live that way. They waste their time and their resources on roads that will never take them where they want to go. They waste years of their lives on highways that don't lead to the destiny God has prepared for them, thinking and talking about things that don't line up with His Word and His will.

Many don't even bother to study the road map He provided in the Bible. If they do, and they happen to get rolling in the right direction, before long they get distracted by something. *Oh, man! That sounds interesting!* they think, and off they go in another direction, devoting their attention to some worldly distraction that, in the long run, won't profit them at all.

In a sense, that's what happened to James. He took his attention off of Jesus and started concerning himself with other things. I don't know for sure what they were. Maybe he got distracted by religious ideas that kept him from accepting his own flesh and blood brother as the Messiah. Maybe he was afraid of looking the fool and losing the respect of his neighbors. After all, nobody else in Nazareth believed Jesus' claims. Intellectual skepticism ran through the town like an interstate and everybody else was on it. So maybe peer pressure pushed James into choosing the same route.

Whatever drove him off course, however, after three years of going nowhere James did something that can inspire us all. He made a U-turn. He cast his fears aside and chose to believe.

Once on the right road, he stayed there. In Acts 2, we find him among the disciples in the upper room praying for the outpouring of the Holy Spirit. In Acts 15, years later, he's advising the elders and apostles of the Jerusalem church, speaking with the voice of authority. In the end, although James missed some opportunities, he refused to let those missed opportunities define him. He didn't let his detour derail his destiny. That's why today nobody remembers James as the brother who blew it or the relative who rejected Jesus.

Instead, his legacy is recorded in the Bible as that of "James, a servant of God and of the Lord Jesus Christ."[27] He holds a place in history and in Scripture as one of the most influential leaders in the early Church. He's remembered as a man who reached His divine destination.

---

[27] James 1:1 NIV

In a way, James reminds me of the athletes on the Wheaties box. They sprinted or swam or drove their race car into the cereal hall of fame not by starting their race well, but by finishing well. In sports as in life, it's how you finish that counts.

For all of us who are still breathing, that's great news because we aren't finished yet. We still have time to make some course corrections. We can still open our Bible and find out how to finish this life like a winner.

Potholes, Armadillos, and Amorites

To be fair, I must warn you that getting on the right road doesn't necessarily guarantee a smooth ride. The devil will see to it that you hit some potholes. He'll throw some tumbleweeds and armadillos under your wheels. (Can you tell I've logged a lot of miles in Texas?)

Even when you're in the perfect will of God, things are going to happen in your life that you may not understand. But don't let those things convince you to change direction. Don't start focusing on what's going wrong. Don't turn your fears into phobias like the lady in the dentist's chair did, dreading disaster until it becomes your destination. Instead, keep your eyes on God, on His promises and His power. Follow Him. Believe His Word. And stay the course.

"But Dennis," somebody might say, "I don't know how to do that! I'm up to my eyeballs in trouble right now. I'm well on my way to being terrified and have no idea what road I'm on."

Don't panic. You're in good company. The greatest people in the Bible found themselves in that condition at one time or another. Take Gideon, for example. When he first appears on the scriptural scene, he'd gone off the road altogether. He was holed up along with his fellow Israelites who were living in mountain caves, quaking in knock-kneed terror of the Midianites and the Amalekites.

And for good reason! According to the Bible:

"Whenever the Israelites planted their crops, marauders from Midian, Amalek, and the people of the east would attack Israel, camping in the land and destroying crops as far away as Gaza. They left the Israelites with nothing to eat, taking all the sheep, oxen, and donkeys. These enemy hordes, coming with their cattle and tents as thick as locusts, arrived on droves of camels too numerous to count. And they stayed until the land was stripped bare. So Israel was reduced to starvation by the Midianites" (Judges 6:3-6 NLT).

Get the picture? We're talking murder, devastation, and starvation on a nationwide scale. I don't know your personal situation, but I'm guessing it's not quite that bad. So it's safe to assume that what Gideon and company did to overcome their problems would also work for you.

They "cried out to the LORD for help" (v. 6).

Calling out to God for assistance is always a good idea. No matter what kind of trouble you've encountered that's the best initial response. The Israelites knew it and I'm sure they hoped God would answer by rolling up His sleeves and making short work of their enemies. They wanted Him to go into action. Drown the Amalekites in a sea. Send a sword-swinging angel to slay the Midianites or scatter them, scurrying and screaming, back from whence they came.

But God didn't do those things. Instead, He simply spoke to them and said:

> *"I brought you up out of slavery in Egypt and rescued you from the Egyptians and from all who oppressed you. I drove out your enemies and gave you their land. I told you, 'I am the LORD your God. You must not worship the gods of the Amorites, in whose land you now live.' But you have not listened to me" (v. 8-10 NLT).*

In other words, God informed Israel that the Midianites and Amalekites were not the problem! The problem was that the Israelites had forgotten His Word. They'd lost sight of what He'd done for them. They were living in dread of an enemy He'd already defeated for them and allowing a conquered foe to rob them of what He'd given them. The Israelites were suffering needless anguish simply because they'd failed to pay attention to what God had already said.

Sound familiar?

Sure it does. As Christians we've done it time and again.

We've trembled in fear at the devil's threats and forgotten that the Bible says that Jesus—our Savior and Champion—*spoiled principalities and powers, and made a show of them openly, triumphing over them.*[28] We've lived like victims of circumstance and forgotten that the New Testament declares, "You are of God, little children, and have overcome them, because He who is in you is greater than he who is in the world" (1 John 4:4). We've put ourselves back in bondage because we haven't fully believed Jesus meant it when He said, "Therefore if the Son makes you free, you shall be free indeed" (John 8:36).

But then, enough about us. Let's get back to Gideon. Where was he in this time of great national trouble?

Threshing wheat at the bottom of a winepress, hoping to hide it from the Midianites.

What a pitiful sight he must have been! Sneezing, coughing, covered head to heel in chaff which, in the windless winepress, clung to him like a dusty second skin. Gideon wasn't focused on his divine destiny. He wasn't thinking about God's promises and power. He was just trying to keep his family from starving to death. He was just struggling to survive. Yet that's the moment the angel of the Lord showed up and said the last thing Gideon ever expected to hear. "The LORD is with you, you mighty man of valor!" (Judges 6:12).

Can't you just see Gideon's face? Slack-jawed. Stupefied. Stunned. He's not only staring eye to eye with a messenger from heaven, he's being introduced to two concepts that never occurred to him in his entire life. First, he's finding out that he's not alone in this mess. The Lord is with him! Second, he's hearing himself described in a way that blows his self-image to smithereens. He's finding out

---

[28] Colossians 2:15

55

that, in the eyes of God, he's a mighty man of valor, a hero, a mighty champion.

The Bible doesn't record that Gideon actually said this, but he had to be thinking it. *Are you sure you have the right guy?*

Drop Your Objections and Believe

Sure enough, the angel had it right. He was delivering the same message to Gideon that God delivers to His born again children throughout the New Testament: *I am with you, mighty champions!*

Amazing as it may seem, that's how God sees us: as new creations in Christ Jesus. Made righteous with His own righteousness. Cleansed with the blood of the Lamb. Delivered out of the power of darkness and into the kingdom of the light of God's Son. Triumphant, overcoming, devil-dominating ambassadors of the Most High God.

"But I don't feel like I'm any of those things."

So what? Stop siding with your emotions and believe your Bible instead. Change your point of view and choose to agree with how God sees you and what He says about you. That's what Gideon did. Well...eventually. First, he tried to get things figured out by asking the angel some questions.

"Sir," Gideon replied, "if the LORD is with us, why has all this happened to us? And where are all the miracles our ancestors told us about? Didn't they say, 'The LORD brought us up out of Egypt'? But now the LORD has abandoned us and handed us over to the Midianites" (v.13 NLT).

To put it bluntly, Gideon was asking why God appeared to have fallen asleep on the job.

Before you keel over in shock at the audacity of such a question, be advised that believers today ask it all the time. "If God is with us, why did dear old, church-going Aunt Mildred get cancer?" they say. "If God is good, why is there so much trouble in the world? If God is loving, why did He let that English lady's momma die in the dentist chair?"

Those sound like deep, theological questions. But they're not. They're proof that people have taken their eyes off God's Word and focused on something else. They're evidence of the kind of thinking that can distract and divert us from our divine destination. The kind of thinking that can literally kill people.

Here's a pearl of wisdom worth remembering: we can't get the right answers by asking the wrong questions. We can't find the right road by staring into the rear-view mirror and asking, "Why did this happen? Why did that happen? Why didn't God intervene? Why? Why? Why?" Questions like that just keep us confused, so God rarely answers them. More often than not He completely ignores them.

In Gideon's case, that's exactly what the angel did. He blew right past his questions and said, "Go with the strength you have, and rescue Israel from the Midianites. I am sending you!" (v. 14 NLT).

Once again, Gideon's mind must have been reeling. *Go in the strength that I have? I don't have any strength! I'm a coward choking on chaff and cowering in a winepress!*

That's how Gideon saw himself. But it's not how God saw him. God saw Gideon as He created him to be. He saw him the same way He sees us—in the light of who He knows He can be in us if we choose to believe Him and move in the direction He is telling us to go!

Had Gideon known this encounter would be recorded in Scripture for eternity, he might have skipped his next argument. He might have saluted the angel and answered like a stalwart soldier of the Lord. "Yes, Sir! Mighty man of valor, at Your service. Look out Midianites, here I come!" But that's not what Gideon did. He insisted on asking a few more questions. Suspecting the less than impressive details of his resume had slipped into the divine sea of forgetfulness, he attempted to jog the memory of the Almighty.

"But Lord," he said, "how can I rescue Israel? My clan is the weakest in the whole tribe of Manasseh, and I am the least in my entire family!" (v. 15 NLT).

Apparently the Creator of the universe doesn't take our family history into account when He designs our destiny. He doesn't alter it because of something that happened to our father or our mother. He doesn't tailor His plan to fit our family tree. So, once again, He ignored Gideon's question and said simply, "I will be with you. And you will destroy the Midianites as if you were fighting against one man" (v. 16 NLT).

At that, Gideon finally dropped his objections. He believed what God said. When he did, it changed his future. It cut short his fears, and they never got to finish their work. As a result, Gideon didn't die young, as he once thought he would, at the hands of his enemies. Instead, he assembled an army and freed his entire nation. He found his way out of the winepress, onto the road to his divine destiny, and departed this earth the way we'd all like to go...*at a good, old age.*[29]

How did Gideon make such a dramatic change? What was his secret? What enabled him to take the step of faith that took him from terror to triumph?

He fixed his thoughts, his dreams, and his faith on these divine facts:

God is with you.

You are a champion.

You will be victorious.

If you're looking for an entrance ramp onto the right road, lock onto those three truths. Meditate on them every single day. Take them with you everywhere (even to the dentist's office). They'll help you find the highway that leads to your God-ordained destination. They'll steer you away from disaster and straight toward your destiny. Not the one you've dreaded, but the one you've dreamed of. The one God planned for you in His great love and goodness before the foundation of the world.

---

[29] Judges 8:32

CHAPTER 4

Redefine Your Identity

Therefore, if anyone is in Christ, he is a new creation; old things have passed away; behold, all things have become new. Now all things are of God, who has reconciled us to Himself through Jesus Christ.

2 Corinthians 5:17-18

Before we leave Gideon and go on to other things, it's only fair to warn you that you probably won't experience exactly what he did. Even if you identify with him, even if you feel that you, too, have spent some time in the winepress of dissatisfaction and defeat, an angel is not likely to show up to help you redefine your identity by telling you you're a champion.

Sorry if that's disappointing, but it's true. Take a survey at church next Sunday and see for yourself. Ask everybody you meet if a celestial messenger has ever barged in on one of their personal pity parties. Ask if they've ever received spectacular angelic assurance that they are far mightier than this world has led them to believe. Odds are, not one single person will say yes.

Why is that? If we, as believers, are destined for greatness, why aren't multitudes of angels being dispatched to tell us so?

Because the message has already been delivered through Someone infinitely greater. It's been sent through Jesus Who, just before He went to the cross, said something absolutely astounding about us. Something recorded in Scripture. Something that, if we will believe it, will redefine our identity just as surely as the angel redefined Gideon's.

Speaking to His heavenly Father about all of us who would ever become His disciples, Jesus said in John 17:16:

"They are not of the world, just as I am not of the world."

"They do not belong to the world, just as I do not belong to the world" (NRSV).

"They are not part of this world any more than I am."

Or, as The Message translation phrases it, "They are no more defined by the world than I am defined by the world."

It's a startling statement in every translation but the last one illuminates it in an especially powerful way, so let's look at it again, personalize it, and let the truth of it sink in. Let's say out loud, "I am no more defined by the world than Jesus is."

It's a staggering concept, isn't it? Maybe that's why most of us—even if we've read that verse many times—haven't really let the truth of it sink in. We've kept it at arm's length by applying it, not to ourselves, but to the original 12 disciples who were standing there when Jesus said it. Because they were the first apostles of the Lamb, it's easy for us to see how He could say such a thing about them. *Yeah,* we think, *they were truly out of this world!*

But the fact is, when the first disciples heard those words, they were a lot like us. They saw themselves as ordinary believers just trying to follow Jesus. They didn't feel like spiritual supermen. So they probably reacted to the Lord's surprising statement much like we would. We don't know for sure because Jesus was praying when He said it and they didn't have a chance to blurt out what they were thinking. They couldn't exactly interrupt His prayer and say, "Excuse me. Could you repeat that, Master? I think I misunderstood You." That would be rude and highly unspiritual. So, most likely, the disciples kept their heads bowed and eyes closed, looking pious on the outside (just like we would) while inside they wondered, *What is He talking about? Anybody can see we're a lot more like the world than He is!*

It would certainly seem like a valid point. After all, Jesus was different from everybody else on earth. He didn't think or function like the rest of society. He didn't adapt to the concepts, the politics, or the religious traditions of the day. He didn't even conform to the circumstances that challenged Him. Operating by the power of God's almighty Spirit, He lived so far above this world order that nothing could dominate Him. He exercised authority over storms, food shortages, demonic spirits, sickness, even death. The disciples had witnessed it all, so it was easy for them to wrap their minds around the idea that He was not of this world.

But for Him to say they were not of this world anymore than He is? No doubt, it was a staggering thought to those first disciples just as it's a staggering thought to us as His disciples today.

Jesus was referring to us too, you know. He made that clear a few verses later when He said, "I do not pray for these alone, but also for those who will believe in Me through their word."[30] Every one of us is born again because we heard, in one way or another, the message the first disciples preached. So when Jesus said, "They are no more defined by the world than I am defined by the world," He was, without question, talking about us!

To *define*, according to the dictionary, means *to identify the essential nature or qualities of something; to set the limits or boundaries of it.* A piece of property can be defined by its latitude and longitude. Its boarders can be determined by its width and length and measured in feet or miles. A container can be defined by how much it can hold. Its capacity can be measured by ounces or gallons.

As human beings, we define ourselves much the same way. We put boundaries around ourselves and borders on how far we think we can go in life. We evaluate our capacity (basing it on what others have said about us or what we've been able to accomplish in the past) and put limits on what we believe God can do through us or for us.

---

[30] John 17:20

But with this one statement, Jesus blasts such boundaries and limits sky high.

"You are no more defined by the world than I am."

Do you realize what that means? It means your past no longer defines your future. It means yesterday's failures don't define your life today. You aren't defined by your education or lack of it, your financial status or your social standing. If you've been divorced, that divorce doesn't define you. If your business went bankrupt, that bankruptcy doesn't define you. The sins and mistakes that are behind you don't limit what's ahead of you.

You've been liberated from all those things. God has turned you loose! He's given you a new identity. He's not defining you based on what you have or have not done. He's not defining you according to your natural assets and abilities. He's defining you based on the potential of what He can be in you and what He can do through you. You've been freed to step into a whole new future. To think bigger than you ever have before. To live on a level that's beyond anything you've ever imagined.

If you think I'm exaggerating, think again. All throughout history, God's people have busted through the boundaries the world tried to set for them. Gideon is just one example. Others abound.

Think about Peter in the book of Acts. Herod locked him up in prison, bound him with chains, and appointed four squads of soldiers to guard him. But the prison didn't define him. (If you've been in prison, it doesn't define you, either. Even if you were there for a different reason.) Peter went to sleep one night behind bars and the next morning, when Herod's minions went to get him, they discovered he'd gone missing. Peter, undefined by a prison sentence, was back out on the streets preaching the Gospel, scot-free.

Think about Joseph in the Old Testament. He was thrown into prison too. Locked up as a slave in a foreign land, the people nearest and dearest to him hated him, betrayed him, and wanted him dead. But Joseph didn't let the prison or the injustice of others define him. He defined himself by the Word of God and his divine dreams—and was promoted from prisoner to Prime Minister overnight.

Think about Moses. He initially misunderstood his assignment. He missed the mark big time by killing an Egyptian and trying to deliver the Hebrews his own way. It was a serious mistake but, in the end, it didn't define him. He ultimately found out what God had in mind, defied the limits of Pharaoh, and liberated a nation of slaves.

And then there was Joshua. He spent 40 years with the Israelites in the wilderness. Yet he never let the wilderness define him. When God told him to rise up and lead the Israelites across the Jordan, he was ready. He went from wilderness wandering to conquering in Canaan, and took possession of the Promised Land.

"But I'm not like any of those people," you might say. "I don't have the divine call on my life they did. I'm not an apostle like Peter, a government leader like Joseph, a prophet like Moses, or a warrior like Joshua. In fact, I don't really know how God defines me."

You can find out by reading Colossians 3:9-11. It says that, as a born again child of God:

"...You have put off the old man with his deeds, and have put on the new man who is renewed in knowledge according to the image of Him who created him, where there is neither Greek nor Jew, circumcised nor uncircumcised, barbarian, Scythian, slave nor free, but Christ is all and in all."

The Message version sums it up this way: "...from now on, everyone is defined by Christ."

Did you get that?

You are defined by Christ! If you want to identify your essential nature and qualities, look at Him. Find out who He is. If you want to determine the boundaries of your life, look at what He can do. Study what He said about you and believe it. Don't limit yourself by the junk the world throws at you; define yourself by who you are in Christ.

Prepare Yourself to Be Peculiar

To redefine yourself in such a revolutionary way you must develop a mindset that's radically different from the world's. You must disregard the opinions of others and renew your mind to think in an entirely new way. But then, that's just part of following Jesus. He's always expected His disciples to do it. Read this passage from Matthew 16 and you'll see what I mean:

"When Jesus came into the region of Caesarea Philippi, He asked His disciples, saying, 'Who

do men say that I, the Son of Man, am?' So they said, 'Some say John the Baptist, some Elijah, and others Jeremiah or one of the prophets.' He said to them, 'But who do you say that I am?' Simon Peter answered and said, 'You are the Christ, the Son of the living God.' Jesus answered and said to him, 'Blessed are you, Simon Bar-Jonah, for flesh and blood has not revealed this to you, but My Father who is in heaven'" (verses 13-17).

Notice Jesus asked His disciples two very different questions. First He asked, "Who do men say that I, the Son of Man, am?"

The disciples answered Him by rehearsing the ideas that were being tossed around by clueless crowds and religious leaders who'd suggested that Jesus was a re-embodiment of John the Baptist, Elijah, Jeremiah, or one of the other prophets. (Isn't that wild? The consensus adopted by the religious Jews of that day centered around the Roman concept of reincarnation. Just goes to show you how the wackiness of the world can creep into church theology.)

The second question Jesus asked—"But who do you say that I am?"—indicated that He assumed the disciples would have a different answer than everyone else did.

He assumes the same about us. He expects us to see Him, and ourselves, and our circumstances in a way that's diametrically opposed to the world's point of view. Much like He asked His first disciples, Jesus still asks us today, "Who does the world say? Who do you say? What's the world saying about the economy? What are you saying about your economy? What does the doctor say about those symptoms you've been experiencing? What's your report?"

Our answers to such questions should be different than the world's answers. We should answer them in the light of what God has to say about those situations. That must become our habit. We must re-train our minds to filter everything through the light of how God, through Christ, has defined us and our reality.

"But, Dennis, if I do that, people will think I'm weird!"

I know. The Bible isn't kidding when it says we're to be a peculiar (set apart or special) people.[31] We're not supposed to think and talk like everybody else. Not that our goal is to be strange, but there's no way around it: if we align ourselves with the truths of the Word and identify ourselves with Jesus, we're going to look odd to the rest of the world.

As Christians, we believe things that to non-Christians are unbelievable. We operate in a system that seems unreasonable to them. For instance, to us it makes perfect sense to give expecting to increase financially because the Bible says, "He who sows sparingly will also reap sparingly, and he who sows bountifully will also reap bountifully."[32] To the world, however, that sounds like crazy talk. They think giving money away makes you poorer, not richer.

---

[31] 1 Peter 2:9: But you are a chosen generation, a royal priesthood, a holy nation, His own special people, that you may proclaim the praises of Him who called you out of darkness into His marvelous light.
[32] 2 Corinthians 9:6

To us, it makes perfect sense to declare we're healed when symptoms of sickness hit because the Bible tells us that healing is ours in Christ and we can have whatsoever we say. To the world, saying you're healed when your body feels sick is denying reality.

I like to compare the system of faith that's ours in Christ to the natural system of aviation. Somebody who knows nothing about airplanes would insist they could never fly. They'd look at a 747 that weighs multiple tons and say, "It's made of metal! It's heavy! If you put it in the air, gravity is going to bring it crashing down."

In some respects, it's a logical argument. Yet every day people get on airplanes and fly all over the world in apparent defiance of gravity. What makes it possible? The laws of lift. A law (or system) that supersedes gravity, the laws of lift make the unreasonable perfectly reasonable. It makes what once seemed impossible a commonplace event.

When I get on an airplane today, expecting it to fly is a no-brainer. I don't even think about the physics of it. I just want to take off so I can ask the flight attendant for a cup of coffee. It never crosses my mind that the plane might fall out of the sky. Because I've learned to define airplanes according to the laws of lift instead of the law of gravity, I can just relax and let the airplane take me where I want to go.

But here is where the analogy ends. When I get on a plane, I can ride on somebody else's revelation. I can sit there passively reading a magazine and enjoying a cup of java because the Wright brothers and many others dared to believe that airplanes could fly. I don't have to study the principles that make it possible. I don't have to develop my own faith in the system. The whole world agrees now that airplanes are a viable form of transportation. So I can just go along with the crowd. I can enjoy the benefits of aviation without much effort at all.

Not so with the spiritual system that's ours through Christ. To operate in that system we must have our own revelation of it. We must study the scriptural truths behind it and develop our faith because the world and the devil are going to oppose us at every turn. Once we decide to define ourselves by Christ, we'll no longer have the luxury of just going along with the world's crowd because from now until the end of this age that crowd will be going the other way.

What Do You Believe?

I realize some people might take issue with those last few statements. They might object to the idea that the redemptive system we, as believers, enjoy sets us apart from the rest of the world. "Ours is a gospel of inclusion!" they might say. "It brings salvation to everyone!"

But that's not what the Bible says. It says, "the gospel of Christ...is the power of God to salvation for everyone *who believes*" (Romans 1:16, emphasis mine).

It's *believing* the gospel that activates God's power for salvation. (Remember, salvation includes more than just missing hell and making heaven. It's God's plan to get some heaven into you so that you can also enjoy some heaven here on earth.) So the real issue, not only

71

for those who are not yet born again, but for those of us who've received Jesus as Lord and Savior, comes down to this: what do you believe?

The only aspects of the gospel that bring change in your life are the aspects you believe in. People who put their faith in Jesus and believe only that He will take them to heaven when they die limit the benefits of their salvation. For them, the gospel becomes little more than an eternal life insurance policy because that's all they believe in. Christians who develop further enjoy additional benefits. For them, the gospel becomes the power of God for protection, healing, prosperity, and other blessings because that's what they believe.

Let me be clear though, true biblical believing doesn't just take place between the ears. Faith isn't just an inert state of mind that assents to a particular truth but does nothing about it. Real faith acts.

Think of it this way. If I was a broker on Wall Street and told you a certain stock was about to quadruple in value, you'd have a decision to make. *Does Dennis know what he's talking about or not?* If you decided my information was reliable and believed it, you'd do something about it. You wouldn't just talk about how deeply you believe what I said. You'd pick up the phone or go online and buy some stock.

The same is true spiritually. You can see what people believe by how they act. They may claim to believe what the Bible says but they don't believe it enough to do anything about it. Which means they don't really believe it at all.

It's easy to nod in agreement and say, "Amen," when we read in the Scripture that we are defined by Christ. It's easy to mentally assent to what Jesus said about our not being defined by this world any more than He is defined by this world. But it takes faith to turn that agreement into action.

"I know it, Dennis," you might say. "And I want to have that kind of faith! But it's a struggle for me."

Look again at Romans 1:16-17 and you'll see something that can help you overcome the struggle.

For I am not ashamed of the gospel of Christ, for it is the power of God to salvation for everyone who believes...For in it the righteousness of God is revealed from faith to faith; as it is written, "The just shall live by faith."

Pay special attention to that last statement. *The just shall live by faith.* It's so short it almost seems inconsequential. Yet the Bible repeats it verbatim again and again:

- Habakkuk 2:4 says, "the just shall live by his faith."

- Galatians 3:11 says, "the just shall live by faith."

- Hebrews 10:38 says, "Now the just shall live by faith."

Many Christians fail in their efforts to live by faith because they've never identified themselves as *the just.* They still see themselves as sinners—saved by grace, yes, but sinners nonetheless—and they assume God sees them that way too. They figure He is as focused on their faults as they are. They can't reach out to Him and receive His blessings because they feel so unworthy and condemned.

It's hard to have faith with that kind of thinking.

And though it's sad to say, Christians have had a lot of help with it. Plenty of ministers and church members, too, see it as their personal responsibility to remind other believers of their failures and sins. Acting as God's little helpers, they do what they can to keep other believers convicted, condemned, down, and defeated.

In reality, of course, they're not God's helpers at all. He doesn't condemn His children. Although He corrects and teaches us as all good fathers do, He doesn't judge us for our shortcomings. He doesn't even see us as sinners anymore. He sees us as possessors of His own righteousness which comes:

> *"By faith of Jesus Christ unto all and upon all them that believe: for there is no difference. For all have sinned, and come short of the glory of God; being justified freely by his grace through the redemption that is in Christ Jesus" (Romans 3:22-24 KJV).*

According to those verses, the moment we believed on Jesus, we were justified. We became *the just*. Gigantic, theological volumes have been written to explain exactly what that means. But, in the end, the concept of justification is best captured by this simple definition often taught to kids in Sunday School: To be justified means *it's-just-as-if-I'd-never sinned.*

Think about that for a moment. What if it was really the story of your life? Where would you be right now if you'd always done everything right? How blessed would you be if you'd always made the right decisions? How successful would you be if every day of your life you'd followed God's plan and never messed up or gotten off track in any way?

I venture to say your life might be a little better. Mine most certainly would be.

Now, consider this: in the mind of God, it really is as if you'd never sinned. The Bible says He remembers your sin no more.[33] Instead, He sees you as born again in the image of Jesus, made righteous on the inside with His own righteousness. And His Spirit is working to reveal that righteousness and justification in a way that transforms your life and makes it truly look like you'd never sinned.

This isn't some kind of pie-in-the-sky theology. This is the real deal for God. He's given us His Word on it and He wants us to stand on that Word. He doesn't want us trying to act all humble by telling Him we're unworthy. He doesn't want us dragging out all our past mistakes and whining about how weak and undeserving we are. Jesus paid the price for us to be free from all that whiney stuff. And God wants us to act on that freedom. He wants us to remind Him not of our past failures, but of our present righteousness. That's why He said:

---

[33] Jeremiah 31:34: "No more shall every man teach his neighbor, and every man his brother, saying, 'Know the LORD,' for they all shall know Me, from the least of them to the greatest of them, says the LORD. For I will forgive their iniquity, and their sin I will remember no more."

"I, even I, am He who blots out your transgressions for My own sake; and I will not remember your sins. Put Me in remembrance; let us contend together; state your case, that you may be acquitted" (Isaiah 43:25-26).

The word *acquitted* is a wonderful word. If you were accused of a crime and taken to court, you'd come out of that courtroom one of two ways. You'd either be found guilty and sentenced to punishment; or you'd be found innocent and acquitted. If you were acquitted, it would be as if you'd never been accused. You'd walk out of the courtroom completely free. You could never be tried for that crime again.

But that's not all. Once the acquittal was handed down, the legal clerks would go to work. They'd go through all the documents that connected you with the crime in any way. They'd blot out your name, wiping out all evidence of the accusation made against you. Your record would be totally expunged.

That's what God did for you through Jesus. He made you "alive together with Him, having forgiven you all trespasses, having wiped out the handwriting of requirements that was against us, which was contrary to us. And He has taken it out of the way, having nailed it to the cross."[34]

---

[34] Colossians 2:13-14

When New Creations Don't Act New

I've always been thrilled that when I was born again, the blood of Jesus canceled out all the sins I'd committed before I was saved. But in my early days as a believer, something still bothered me. I wasn't sure how God handled the sins I committed after I became a Christian. Did He just wipe my past record clean, make me a new creation, and then start a fresh tally of my sins? And if so, how did my post-salvation sins affect my status as a believer?

That's actually something we all need to know because even though we're new creations, we don't always act all that new. Sometimes we stumble back into our old habits. Apparently God knew it was going to happen because He told us in the Bible what to do about it. He said if we sin, we can confess it to Him and He will be "faithful and just to forgive us our sins and to cleanse us from all unrighteousness."[35]

What's more, the New Testament makes it abundantly clear that the sins we stumble into after we're born again don't change who we are. They don't turn us back into "sinners" again. I found that out years ago by studying Paul's letter to the Romans. Noting each time Paul used the word *sin* in one form or another, I discovered that 47 times it's used as a noun. I'm no grammar expert but I do know this: a noun refers to a person, place, or thing. In Romans, the majority of the time, sin refers to a place.

The way I envision it, the place of sin is like a cage. Because of Adam and the sinful nature that was passed

---

[35] 1 John 1:9

77

down to us as a result of his disobedience in the Garden of Eden, all mankind ended up in the sin cage. We had no power to free ourselves. Then Jesus came and unlocked the cage by paying sin's penalty. The moment we put our faith in Him, we stepped out of the place of sin and into the place of righteousness or justification.

The problem is many believers don't understand that. They've been brainwashed by the devil and religion to believe that, despite their faith in Jesus, they're still in the sin cage. They look back at the iron bars and remember all the bad things they've done. They sing songs in church about how they're just old sinners saved by grace (which, by the way, is impossible; you're either a sinner or you're saved by grace, but you can't be both). They feel like they don't deserve to live outside the cage so they go back inside it and live like prisoners even though Jesus has set them free.

Other believers have a slightly different experience. They celebrate their freedom. They step out of the place of sin and, for a while, enjoy the place of righteousness. But then they mess up. They miss it. They sin. In this case, sin becomes a verb or an action word.

In Romans, the verb form of sin is used seven times. But here's where the news gets really good. The verb (or action) of sin can never put us, as believers, back in the noun (or place) of sin. It's impossible! For an action of sin to return us to the place of sin and make us sinners again, that action would have to be mightier than the blood of Jesus—and no act of sin is that powerful!

Look at it this way. Before you were born again, when you were still locked up in the sinner's cage, you couldn't do enough good actions to free yourself. You couldn't work your way out of the place of sin. The reverse is also true. Once you've been delivered from the sin place through redemption, you can't by negative actions work your way back in.

What Jesus did for you on Calvary is far greater than your failures can ever be. His righteousness that's yours by faith trumps anything you could ever do wrong. "Therefore if the Son makes you free, you shall be free indeed."[36]

If you want to define yourself by Christ, start here: You are the just. In the eyes of God, it's just-as-if-you-never-sinned. You aren't trying to work your way into righteousness, you're already there—not because of what you've done but because of what you believe.

As disciples of Jesus, you and I don't have to wonder anymore whether or not we can qualify to receive the blessings of God. Instead, we can spend our time:

"Giving thanks to the Father who has [already!] qualified us to be partakers of the inheritance of the saints in the light. He has delivered us from the power of darkness and conveyed us into the kingdom of the Son of His love, in whom we have redemption through His blood, the forgiveness of sins" (Colossians 1:12-14).

---

[36] John 8:36

This is literally the gospel truth. Jesus has blown your former limitations sky high. He doesn't have to send an angel to tell you about it either. He delivered the message Himself. He included you when he said, "They are no more defined by the world than I am defined by the world." And with those words, He gave you more than Gideon ever dreamed of. So go on, mighty hero of valor, get out of the winepress and live.

CHAPTER 5

Get a New Tattoo

*...Stop assuming an outward expression that does
not come from within you and is not representative
of what you are in your inner being but is patterned
after this age; but change your outward expression
to one that comes from within and is representative
of your inner being, by the renewing of your mind.*

Romans 12:2 Wuest

I don't have a tattoo. And, not being a tattoo kind of guy,
I have no plans to get one. But I am certain of this. If I
ever decided to brand myself with something, it definitely
wouldn't be the phase *Born to Lose*.

Not to say that gives me any special bragging rights.
Most normal people (tattoo aficionados included) would
prefer to avoid marking themselves with such negativ-
ity. Not everybody though. At least, according to the late
Norman Vincent Peale.

He used to tell the story of a time when, on a business trip to Hong Kong, he was walking down the narrow, twisted streets in the old part of the city and a tattoo studio caught his attention. Peering in the window, he studied the display of choices available to interested customers. There, among the anchors, flags, mermaids, and various Chinese symbols, he saw one choice—advertised in English—that mystified him.

Curious, Peale stepped inside the shop and found an aging Chinese tattoo artist. "Excuse me," he said. "I couldn't help but notice you offer a tattoo that reads *Born to Lose*. Does anybody ever ask for that one? Do people actually have those words inscribed on their body?"

The elderly man nodded. "Sometimes, they do," he answered. Then, noting Peale's astonished expression, the man tapped his forehead and added in broken English, "But tattoo on mind before tattoo put on body."

Tattoo on mind. That's something that can be said about all of us. Whether or not we're inclined to have pictures and slogans imprinted on our anatomy, on the inside we're all tattooed. Our minds are engraved with images and phrases that describe who we think we are. For better or for worse, we all adopt certain definitions of ourselves, and those definitions determine the boundaries of our lives.

In Chapter 4, we saw that Jesus said to those of us who are in Him, our boundaries are limitless. As His disciples, we're not defined by this world any more than He is. As Colossians 3:11 says, we are defined by Christ.

Without question, those are thrilling statements. They're wonderful to read and exciting to talk about. But here's the bottom line reality. In your life, in your own personal experience, it's not just what Jesus says or what the Bible says that matters. It's what you say that makes the ultimate difference.

So, let me ask you something. Who are you, and what do you say about yourself?

Those may sound like peculiar questions, but actually they're quite scriptural. They're the questions the priests and Levites from Jerusalem asked John the Baptist when, having heard about him and his unusual ministry, they showed up at his revival in the wilderness to check him out. John had so defied their cultural norms (eating questionable fare, wearing hair suits, and preaching things that made them uncomfortable) they felt he owed them explanation. "Who are you?" they demanded.

Assuming he'd claim to be the Messiah, they must have been disappointed by his response. "I am not the Christ," he said.

"What then? Are you Elijah?" they asked.

"I am not."

"Are you the Prophet?"

"No."

"Well, then who are you...?" they asked. "What do you say about yourself?"

John's answer was a stunner: "I am 'the voice of one crying in the wilderness: "Make straight the way of the LORD,"' as the prophet Isaiah said" (John 1:19-23).

With that reply, John the Baptist set the standard. He provided an example that every believer can follow. He didn't define himself by giving his opinion. He didn't rehearse his past, or repeat what his parents and peers said about him. He didn't base his reply on natural circumstances, appearances, his family, his upbringing, or his educational status.

John, being just as human as we are, could certainly have chosen to describe himself in those terms. But he didn't. Instead, he defined his identity with the Scriptures. He said in essence, "I have found myself in the Word of God, and I am saying of myself what God has said about me."

Granted, John the Baptist was a unique individual. Given his special place in Biblical history and his well-known idiosyncrasies, we might chalk him up as one of a kind. We might be tempted to shrug off his example if it wasn't for this: Jesus said exactly the same kind of thing.

All through His ministry, people asked Him, just as they asked John, "Who are you?"[37] Especially at the beginning when He went to preach in Nazareth where He'd been brought up, that question was at the forefront of everybody's mind. The townsfolk of Nazareth had always known Jesus as a friend or relative or neighbor. To them He was just a home town boy. The reports about Him teaching in all the surrounding synagogues with

---

[37] John 8:25

power and authority sounded strange to them. So when He came to town, they gathered in the synagogue to hear with their own ears what Jesus had to say about Himself.

The fourth chapter of Luke tells what happened.

"....As His custom was, He [Jesus] went into the synagogue on the Sabbath day, and stood up to read. And He was handed the book of the prophet Isaiah. And when He had opened the book, He found the place where it was written: 'The Spirit of the LORD is upon Me, because He has anointed Me to preach the gospel to the poor; He has sent Me to heal the brokenhearted, to proclaim liberty to the captives and recovery of sight to the blind, to set at liberty those who are oppressed; to proclaim the acceptable year of the LORD.' Then He closed the book, and gave it back to the attendant and sat down. And the eyes of all who were in the synagogue were fixed on Him. And He began to say to them, 'Today this Scripture is fulfilled in your hearing'" (verses 16-21).

To understand what Jesus did here, you have to realize, He didn't just stumble onto these verses in Isaiah by accident. He found them. He sought them out on purpose because He'd long ago discovered His identity in them. By reading them, He was saying about Himself what God said. He was defining Himself by the Word.

The people who were listening had no clue what He was doing. As devout Jews, they'd heard Isaiah read many times before and they didn't expect it to sound different just because Jesus was reading it. But somehow it did. Something about the way He said those scriptures so startled the congregation that when Jesus finished reading and sat down, everybody stared at Him, waiting for an explanation.

The one He gave shocked them even more. "Isaiah was talking about Me when he wrote this," He said. "I'm the One who's anointed to preach the gospel to the poor, heal the brokenhearted, bring sight to the blind, and set the oppressed free. The power of God is available to you all right now because I'm here and that power is on Me."

The sermon wasn't well received.

By the time Jesus finished what He had to say, the crowd was seething. "Isn't this Joseph's son?" they said. "Is this not the carpenter, the son of Mary, and brother of James, Joses, Judas, and Simon? And are not his sisters here with us?"[38] The very idea that Jesus claimed to be anointed made the bunch at Nazareth so mad that they mobbed him and took Him to the top of a nearby cliff, intending to push Him off.

Not exactly the kind of response a young minister hopes to receive the first time he preaches in his home town. But Jesus knew how to handle it. Passing through the midst of them, He simply went on His way.

The Word Activates the Power

Even though Jesus made it safely out of town, you might wonder why He chose to say what He did to the folks that day. Why didn't He soften His message a little?

---

[38] Mark 6:3

Surely He knew they'd have trouble processing His Messianic identity. These were His old friends and neighbors. They'd seen Him as a child playing tag with the other kids. They'd seen Him in His carpentry shop with sleeves rolled up and sawdust in His hair.

Couldn't He have said something a little more palatable? Couldn't He have toned things down a bit?

No, He couldn't. Jesus doesn't use words the way the world does. He doesn't just say what people want to hear or what He feels like saying. He speaks the Word of God because that Word activates God's power.

It wasn't in Jesus' heart to be hard on those people. He'd known and loved them all His life. He wanted to minister to them. He wanted to heal them and set them free. But to do it, He had to operate in the power of God's anointing. And to activate that anointing, He had to speak the Word. He had to say about Himself what God said.

If they'd believed Him, wonderful things would have happened. Cousin Mildred could have been healed of the arthritis that had crippled her for years. Uncle Harry could have been delivered from the demons that dogged him. Miracles could have been the order of the day. But the folks in Nazareth missed out. Instead of believing Jesus' words, they were offended by them. As a result, "He could do no mighty work there, except that He laid His hands on a few sick people and healed them. And He marveled because of their unbelief."[39]

What does all that have to do with us?

---

[39] Mark 6:5-6

Think again about what Jesus said in John 17:15. We're not of this world any more than He is. That means we're supposed to use our words not like the world does but like Jesus did. We're supposed to activate God's anointing in us and upon us by believing what God says about us and declaring it to be true.

I don't know why so many Christians think that's such a bizarre idea. The fact is, everybody who's born again has already done it. That's how we got saved. We activated God's power for salvation in our life by believing in our heart and confessing with our mouth that Jesus is our Lord.

But somehow we got the idea that an act of faith and confession was supposed to be a one-time event. We saw it as something we do just to get into the kingdom of God. But actually it's the way the entire kingdom works. Believing and declaring God's Word is the way we access and release His power every day of our lives. It's what causes God's will to be done on earth as it is in heaven.

What we say is so important that the New Testament calls Jesus the Apostle and High Priest of our confession.[40] He's the One appointed and anointed to bring to pass our words of faith. But He can't do His job if what we say is contrary to the Bible.

So, let me ask you again. Who are you and what are you saying about yourself?

If you're like most believers, a lot of what you believe and say about yourself is negative. The world has trained

---

[40] Hebrews 3:1

you that way. I've heard the most wonderful, God-loving, devoted saints say things about themselves that flatly contradict the Word. They'll make a mistake and mutter, "Oh, man! I'm just so stupid! I'm always messing things up! I just can't get anything right these days!"

What's wrong with that?

Mark 11:23, that's what. There Jesus said whatever we believe in our heart and say with our mouth is what we'll have.

Oops.

I don't mind telling you, I used to be as bad about it as anybody. I'd say whatever negative thought came to mind. But I changed when I discovered what the Bible says about me and began spending time with believers who'd cultivated the habit of using their words the way God intended. Just a few years working and fellowshipping with Kenneth Copeland, for example, revolutionized my vocabulary. He absolutely believes Jesus meant it when He said, "by your words you will be justified, and by your words you will be condemned," and he speaks accordingly. Not just when he's in church but all the time.

I'll never forget when a few of us were on a motorcycle trip together and my good friend Jesse Duplantis stuck his foot in his mouth right in front of Brother Copeland. We'd stopped to spend the night in Cody, Wyoming. Our wives had gone into the hotel to get cleaned up for dinner while Jesse, Brother Copeland, and I wrapped up the bikes for the night.

As we finished up, we were standing there talking when Jesse—who'd already put the cover over his motor-cycle—suddenly looked at me and said, "Dennis, I forgot to lock down my bike!"

I smiled a little, knowing this wasn't the first time he'd done it. We'd been on the road for five days and he'd forgotten to lock his bike every single night. I didn't mention it, but Jesse did.

"I always forget to lock down that bike!" he said. "I always forget it!"

Brother Copeland grinned at me. "Yeah, and he just set himself up to do it again."

Exasperated with himself, Jesse shook his head. "Man! This confession stuff is killing me!" Kenneth and I just stood there looking at each other, so tickled we could hardly breathe.

"And I can't believe I just said that in front of Kenneth Copeland!" Jesse added.

We laughed so hard we almost fell on the ground.

Just Say What You Believe

What makes Jesse's mistake so funny is we've all made it. We've all developed verbal habits we fall into without even thinking about it. So we know how Jesse felt. And while it's okay to laugh at him—he wouldn't mind, he loves to make people laugh—we must also remember this is a serious matter. Our words are no joke. When we use them to declare how sick we are, or how broke we are, or what losers we are, our words can be deadly.

I shudder when I hear believers say things like this: "Alcoholism just runs in my family. I've always had trouble with it and I always will. It's just in my genes." Or "Every man in our family died at 52 years old. My father, grandfather, and great-grandfather all died at that age. I'm 49 now and I've already picked out my burial plot because I figure I only have three years left."

I'm not kidding. I've heard Christians say those things and it's a tragedy because words like that kill our faith. They kill our future. They fill our lives with the curse instead of the blessing and promises of God.

I realize some people don't want to hear that. It upsets them. They get legalistic about it and miss the revelation behind it. They stress out trying to ride both sides of the fence. "I don't want to make the wrong confession," they say, "but...I'm just feeling terrible. I don't have the money to pay my bills. It seems like my mind is failing me. I can't remember anything these days. Things are just going from bad to worse."

"But Dennis, that's what the situation looks like. I can't figure out what else to say."

It's really not all that difficult. Just say what God says. Just say what you believe.

How are you going to find out what to believe?

The same way John the Baptist did. He had to pour over Scripture, being led by the Spirit, until he found the statement in the Book of Isaiah that defined his identity. Once he found it, he had to treat it like more than just a Bible verse. He had to receive it as a Word from God about who he was. He had to agree with it, believe it, and say it about himself.

"Yeah, but John the Baptist was a great prophet!"

So what? He still could have doubted God's words. He could have acted like we do sometimes and questioned if he was really what the Bible said he was. He could have wondered, *Is that really talking about me? Am I truly the voice of one crying in the wilderness? I don't know if I really qualify for such a calling. Sometimes I don't feel like I measure up. Do I really have what it takes?*

Everybody grapples with those kinds of thoughts. When we look at our own natural weaknesses and inabilities, we all feel like we fall short of what the Word says about us. But it doesn't matter. We don't have to live up to our scriptural identity on our own. When we embrace that identity by faith and declare it as fact, God's power goes to work in us to enable and empower us to be everything He has said we are.

Philippians 2:13 puts it this way: "...it is God who works in you both to will and to do for His good pleasure."

That's a verse you'll want to remember because just like John the Baptist, you've been called to do things far beyond anything you can do in your own strength. You have a divine destiny that's been mapped out by God to reflect His definition of you. And He doesn't define you by your natural talents and skills. He doesn't define you by your fleshly limitations or shortcomings. Because you're in Jesus and Jesus is in you, He defines you by Christ.

The more you find out about what that means and the more you believe it, the more God's definition of you will become a reality in your daily life. So, if you aren't doing it already, start studying the Bible in a fresh way. Look into God's Word not just to learn about God but to learn about yourself.

It never occurs to most Christians to study the Scriptures with that perspective. Even Bible schools don't encourage it. They focus for the most part on the history of Israel and the church. They teach facts about God, on who He is and what He's done. But they neglect to emphasize what the Bible says about us as His family and His children. Very little teaching time is spent on who we are in Him.

That's why so many Christians are living in defeat.

- They can't enjoy victory over the sin in their lives because they haven't been taught that their old man—the sin-dominated fleshly person they were before they got born again—was crucified with Christ. They don't know that the Bible says, "Your old evil desires were nailed to the cross with him; that part of you that loves to sin was crushed and fatally wounded, so that your sin-loving body is no longer under sin's control, no longer needs to be a slave to sin" (Romans 6:6 TLB).

- They can't enjoy victory over sickness because they don't realize when Jesus went to the cross, He not only bore their sins, He also took away their sicknesses and pains. They don't know that by His stripes they were healed.[41]

- They can't enjoy victory over lack because they don't know that, according to God's definition, through Jesus they've been made rich.[42] They don't grasp the fact that God will supply all their needs—not according to the meagerly resources of the worldly economy, not according to what their employer is willing to pay them—but according to the riches in glory by Christ Jesus.[43]

- They suffer from insecurity and rejection because they don't see themselves as God sees them: as completely and wonderfully accepted in the Beloved.[44]

Don't misunderstand me. I'm not blaming the Church's lack of knowledge just on Bible schools. I appreciate them and the education they provide. I've gone to Bible school myself and I'm grateful for Bible teachers everywhere—in classrooms, churches, home groups, or anywhere else—who help people study the Scriptures from a historical point of view. But in the end, for our Christianity to really matter, that history has to come alive in us so that we see the power of God in the here and now. What God has done in the past must become what God is doing in our own lives in the present. Otherwise, the gospel ceases to be good news and simply becomes old news.

---

[41] 1 Peter 2:24
[42] 2 Corinthians 8:9
[43] Philippians 4:19
[44] Ephesians 1:6

Remember the fossilized church I told you about? The one I visited not long after I got born again? The congregation there had no life in it because in their minds the Bible was about what happened, not about what's happening. The people in those pews probably knew a lot about what happened in Jesus' ministry 2,000 years ago. They knew who He was, what He did, and what He said about Himself.

But it's not just who Jesus was and what He did a couple of millennia ago that keeps the kingdom of God alive and advancing in this day and age. It's not just what He said about Himself back then that makes His power available to people today. The present day ministry of Jesus depends on us. It's who we are through our relationship with Him and what we say about ourselves today that opens the door for Him to work now—not only in our lives but in the world as well.

That's the reason Jesus gave us the Great Commission. That's why, among His last words to us as His disciples, were these:

"All authority has been given to Me in heaven and on earth. Go therefore and make disciples of all the nations, baptizing them in the name of the Father and of the Son and of the Holy Spirit, teaching them to observe all things that I have commanded you; and lo, I am with you always, even to the end of the age" (Matthew 28:18-20).

Notice, Jesus didn't say that He was going to go preach and make disciples and we could tag along. He said, "You do it and I'll go with you." Jesus didn't say in Mark 16 that signs and healings would follow Him. He said, "The signs will follow you who believe."

As inadequate as we may sometimes feel, we as believers are now Jesus' hands and feet on the earth. We are His mouthpiece.

We are *the body of Christ.*

Sometimes we miss the significance of that statement because we don't fully understand the word *Christ*. It's a Greek word that literally translated means the Anointed One and/or the anointing. During Jesus' earthly ministry, the anointing of God was on only one Person. So the body of Christ was singular. But today the body of Christ is plural. It's made up of many members, and we all have the anointing of Jesus.

When we understand that, all of a sudden what Jesus said about Himself in Luke 4 becomes very personal and extremely significant. We find ourselves in His words, just like He found Himself in the words of the prophet Isaiah. Because we are in Christ and He is in us we can say of ourselves the same thing He said.

"The Spirit of the Lord is upon me, _____(insert your name), because He has anointed me to preach the gospel to the poor; He has sent me to heal the brokenhearted, to proclaim liberty to the captives and recovery of sight to the blind, to set at liberty those who are oppressed; to proclaim the acceptable year of the LORD."

I know those are bold things to say about the likes of you and me but they're true. The calling and assignment that belonged to Jesus now belongs to us. He is the Anointed One and we are the Anointed Ones.

When we begin to meditate on that truth and let it spring to life inside us, we'll start seeing ourselves in a new light. When we pray, we'll expect things to happen. When we minister in Jesus' name we'll expect demons to flee, bodies to be healed, and circumstances to change.

Not just when we're in church, either. The anointing isn't just for church services. Jesus proved that beyond any doubt. When he was at a wedding and the hosts ran out of refreshments, He released the anointing, turned water into wine, and kept the party going. When he passed a funeral procession and saw a widow grieving her only son, he reached out with the anointing and raised the boy from the dead. When He was walking near a cemetery and a crazy, naked, demon-possessed man who lived among the tombs made a rush at Him, Jesus spoke anointed words and, long story short: the demons fled. The man got his sanity back. And he left the cemetery with his clothes on looking for a better place to live.

It's amazing stuff...all of it.

And none of it happened in church.

Stay Armed and Dangerous

Am I suggesting that we, as members of the body of Christ, can do such things? No, I'm not suggesting it. I'm saying it outright. We are called and anointed to do the works Jesus did and even greater.[45]

---

[45] John 14:12

To do those works, however, our minds must be renewed to the revelation of who we are in Him. And that's not something that happens in an instant. It's a process. A process that requires discipline and diligence. A process that involves getting up every day and putting on a new mentality, reminding ourselves that we're not the old sinner we used to be but a "new man...created according to God, in true righteousness and holiness."[46]

We must put on our new-man-thinking daily, like we put on our clothes. We can never afford to be without it because as long as we live in this natural world we'll find ourselves confronted with contrary evidence. We'll see things and hear things and feel things that seem to indicate we're not as victorious and anointed as the Bible says we are. We'll have to deal with a devil that assaults our minds with destructive thoughts and tries to define us according to his lies.

Once we decide to take our position in Christ, the forces of darkness will do everything they can to wrestle us out of it. So we have to stay armed and dangerous, ready to disrupt Satan's strategies and our low-level thinking with thoughts straight from God's Word.

In Ephesians 6, Paul compares it to equipping ourselves for battle. He tells us to fasten the truth around our minds like a belt so that our identity in Christ can't slip away from us. To put on righteousness like a breastplate and guard our hearts against guilt and condemnation so that when the devil comes to accuse us we can say,

[46] Ephesians 4:23-24

"No! I'm forgiven! I'm right in God's sight! He's cleansed me and made me just as if I'd never sinned."

Paul tells us to put on the helmet of salvation and guard our thinking so that when we run into trouble and we're tempted to think we're going to fail, we can resist him with the Word. We can say without hesitation, "I'm not a failure, I'm an overcomer. I can do all things through Christ who strengthens me."

To make such declarations with real conviction, you have to know for yourself that they're true. You can't depend just on what preachers and other Christians say. You have to do what John the Baptist and Jesus did. Find yourself in the Word. Don't take somebody else's word for it. Search the Scriptures and see for yourself what God says about you.

If you're not sure where to begin, start with the epistles of Paul. He had more revelation about our identity in Christ than any other biblical writer. Get a highlighter and read through books like Romans, Ephesians, Philippians, and Colossians, marking every verse that says something about who you are in Christ, what you have through Him, and what His Spirit within you empowers you to do.

Make a list of those things. Read them aloud every day until they become an automatic part of your vocabulary. Say them until you're not just "making a positive confession" but declaring what you've discovered for yourself in the Word. Get them down inside you until you can say them not only because they're in the Bible but because you believe them with all your heart.

In other words, tattoo yourself with the truth. Not on the outside but on the inside.

That's something we all have to do if we want to live the way Jesus intended, because somewhere in our past, in one way or another, the devil branded us all as Born to Lose. It's a rotten inscription, but thank God, it's not indelible. It can be blotted out with the blood of Jesus and the Word of God. It can be replaced with another, more eternal brand. A tattoo worth wearing forever:

Born to Give Glory to God.

CHAPTER 6

Learn the Lesson of Limitless Living

...With God all things are possible.

Matthew 19:26

If it happened today, few people would ever hear about it. The local paper wouldn't cover it. Neither would the evening news. The only publications daring enough to mention it would be the tabloid variety. There, next to the reported sightings of Elvis and aliens, you might find an article headlined: Preacher Feeds 20,000 at Stadium Service with a Single Happy Meal.

The article wouldn't be taken seriously, of course. Satisfying a hungry crowd the size of a small town with a few dozen French fries and a burger the size of a silver dollar is impossible, and most everybody knows it.

Everybody except Jesus, that is. He not only believes it's possible, He did it.

All four writers of the New Testament gospels reported the miracle. Matthew, Mark, Luke, and John all tell the story of how Jesus fed some 20,000-plus people with a small basket of food. Granted, the details were slightly different than they would be today. Instead of serving up His banquet in a stadium, Jesus provided it picnic-style on a hillside in Galilee. Instead of starting with a Happy Meal, He used five small loaves of bread and a couple of small fish.

But the result was the same. He took the mundane and made it miraculous. He defied impossibilities. He ignored the limitations most of us live by, and showed us how—by faith in the power of God working in us and through us—we can redefine ourselves and our reality.

Personally, I'm convinced that's the primary reason Jesus fed the multitudes: to give us a lesson in limitless living. He wanted us to see what can happen when we refuse to bow to the boundaries set by circumstances and natural human reasoning. He wanted to reveal how He operates so that we can do it too.

That's why He involved His disciples in the miracle. If He'd only been interested in feeding the crowd, He could have done it all by Himself. But He brought the disciples in on the action to teach them (and us) four vital principles that, when put into operation, will redefine any situation. Four keys that can transform the most overwhelming circumstance and turn us into the overcomers God has called us to be.

The sixth chapter of John's gospel tells us how the process unfolded. It says:

"After these things, Jesus went over the Sea of Galilee, which is the Sea of Tiberias. Then a great multitude followed Him, because they saw His signs which He performed on those who were diseased. And Jesus went up on the mountain, and there He sat with His disciples. Now the Passover, a feast of the Jews, was near. Then Jesus lifted up His eyes, and seeing a great multitude coming toward Him, He said to Philip, 'Where shall we buy bread, that these may eat?'" (verses 1-5).

When Jesus asks a question, He's never looking for information. He wasn't asking Philip where to buy bread because He'd run out of ideas. Jesus wasn't in need of suggestions. He'd already settled the fact that He was going to feed these people. He was just giving Philip an opportunity to disclose his frame of mind. He was saying, in essence, *Hey, Philip, what's your perspective on this situation?*

Suddenly, Philip was on the hot seat. All eyes were turned in his direction. He wanted to say something wise, something anointed. Determined to get this right, beads of sweat may have glistened on his forehead as he pondered his answer. But all he could think to say was, "Two hundred denarii worth of bread is not sufficient for them, that every one of them may have a little!"[47]

To Philip it seemed like an important and relevant observation. After all, a denarii equaled a full day's wage

[47] Verse 7

for an average worker, so 200 denarii was a lot of money. But that had nothing to do with Jesus' question. He didn't ask if they had enough money to buy bread for everybody. He asked *where* they should buy the bread.

Philip never even heard the word *where*. He was too preoccupied with the masses of people and the vastness of the need. All he could see was the money problem. Trapped in the mentality of insufficiency, his brain spun like a hamster on a wheel covering the same ground again and again. *It would take almost a year's wages to buy bread for these people, and even then, everybody would only get a microscopic amount. Jesus, you have to be kidding!*

But Jesus wasn't kidding. The look on His face must have made that clear because one of the other disciples piped up with another idea. Andrew said, "There is a lad here who has five barley loaves and two small fish..."

Too bad Andrew didn't stop there. He could have gone down in scriptural history as a giant of faith. But his perspective was as limited as Philip's. His eyes were on the scarcity of the supply instead of the greatness of God's power. So his declaration which started out with a bang ended with a whimper. "Here's a kid with some loaves of bread and fish...*but what are they among so many?*"

The rest of the disciples played it safe and kept quiet. They just stood there staring at the crowd and this one basket of food, agreeing silently with Philip and Andrew, thinking, *This isn't enough! We can't afford to feed this many people!* They, too, had totally forgotten Jesus' original question, "Where shall we buy bread that these may eat?" It seemed so ridiculous they just shrugged it off. Even if they'd tried to answer it, the only correct answer would have been, "Nowhere! There isn't a bakery within miles big enough to provide the kind of meal You have in mind, Jesus. No matter how much money we have, we can't buy that much bread."

Actually, I think the Lord would have liked that answer. It would have opened the door for Him to make His point, to tell them, "It's not about what you can buy, it's about what you can believe. It's not about finances, it's about faith. When your confidence is in God, impossibilities are no problem because *all things are possible to him who believes.*"[48]

Jesus didn't say those things right then because the disciples were too locked into the lack mentality to understand them. He chose instead to teach by illustration. "Bring the loaves and fish here to Me,"[49] He said. And with that command, He revealed the first key to limitless living.

Give Jesus Something to Work With

This is God's pattern all through the Bible. He expects us to participate in our miracle by taking something we have—no matter how inadequate it may seem—and giving it to Him. Like the loaves and fish, what we have may not be much, but when we put it in the hands of Jesus, it becomes a seed He can bless and multiply until it meets the need.

[48] Mark 9:23
[49] Matthew 14:18

The Scriptures give us numerous examples of how this principle works. One of my favorites is the Old Testament story about the widow of Zarephath. Talk about somebody who was hungry! This lady wasn't like the multitudes Jesus fed. She hadn't just missed a meal or two because she'd been at church all day. She was literally starving. Having mixed together her last smidgeon of flour and oil, she'd made one last little cake for herself and her son so they could eat it and die.

Her plan was interrupted, however, when the prophet Elijah showed up on her doorstep and made an utterly audacious request. "Don't be afraid! Go ahead and cook that 'last meal,' but bake me a little loaf of bread first," he said. "Afterward there will still be enough food for you and your son."[50]

To us, that may sound reasonable. After all, Elijah was a great, miracle-working prophet of God. But this widow wasn't even an Israelite. She didn't know what God would do for her. It's a wonder that she didn't tell Elijah to take a hike. But for some reason she didn't. Instead, she did exactly what he asked. She took her last little bit of cake mix, cooked it up, and put it into the hands of the prophet.

She gave God something to work with.

"...And she and Elijah and her son continued to eat from her supply of flour and oil for many days. For no matter how much they used, there was always enough left in the containers, just as the LORD had promised through Elijah."[51]

[50] 1 Kings 7:13 NLT
[51] Verses 15-16 NLT

This is often the way it is in God's system. What He tells us to do doesn't always make sense to our head. According to natural reasoning it seems crazy to give when we're already in a financial hole. It looks to us like giving money away will get us in the hole even deeper. But that's not true. When we give tithes and offerings, we shift our thinking off of our need and onto our provider. We put something in God's hands that He can work with—something He can multiply and increase until we "always having all sufficiency in all things...have an abundance for every good work."[52]

Finances aren't the only things we can put into God's hands, of course. We can also give Him our time, our prayers, our attention, and our obedience. Apart from God's touch, such things may seem as ordinary as the contents of the little boy's basket. They may look as inadequate as a handful of crescent rolls and a couple of perch. But when we bring what we have to Jesus, the extraordinary happens. He takes the natural things we give Him, blesses them, uses them, and creates a supernatural result.

Sit Down...Expecting

Once the disciples had given Jesus something to work with, He revealed the second principle of limitless living by giving another simple command. He said:

"Make the people sit down" (John 6:10).

---

[52] 2 Corinthians 9:8

Sitting down doesn't sound like any big deal, I know. But in this case it's super significant because it illustrates what we all must do to see the miraculous happen in our lives. We must enter a place of rest. We must realize it's not our performance that causes God to act on our behalf. It's not keeping all the rules. It's not wearing ourselves out doing a lot of good works that opens the door to His blessing in our lives—it's our faith. And real faith in God puts us at rest.

Hebrews 4:3-4 says it this way, "For we who have believed do enter that rest...For He [God] has spoken in a certain place of the seventh day in this way: 'And God rested on the seventh day from all His works.'"

Let me ask you something. Have you ever wondered why God rested on the seventh day of creation? Certainly it wasn't because He was tired. The Bible says God never gets weary.[53] Why then did He rest? Because He was finished with His work. There was nothing more for Him to do. The work of creation was complete.

As it turned out, God's initial rest didn't last very long. As soon as Adam sinned and messed things up, God got back on the job. That's why Jesus said during His ministry on earth, "My Father has been working until now, and I have been working."[54] The Father and Son were laboring together to bring forth the plan of redemption and restore the place of divine fellowship and dominion to mankind that they had in the beginning.

---

[53] Isaiah 40:28
[54] John 5:17

After Jesus' crucifixion and resurrection, the work of redemption was finished. Once He was raised from the dead and seated at the right hand of God (having raised us up with Him and seated us together with Him in heavenly places), God returned to His rest and invited us to join Him.

Now, we can rest by faith in what Jesus has done. Unlike the people who lived under the Old Covenant, we don't have to strive and labor and do...do...do in order to earn God's blessing. Jesus earned it for us. When we put our faith in Him, we step into the day of rest. We enter into God's finished work of redemption where healing is ours, prosperity is ours, and every promise in the Bible has been fulfilled for us in Christ Jesus.

Through the New Covenant we have a new operating system. It's a system of faith and grace; of righteousness, not performance. It's a system of walking in peaceful calm instead of racking our brains wondering, *Have I prayed enough? Have I shared Jesus enough? Have I read my Bible enough?* When we think that way, our eyes are on ourselves and not on the Master. We wear ourselves out wondering whether we're worthy. But, thank God, we don't have to live like that anymore.

Spiritually, we can do what the hungry multitude did on the mountainside. We can sit down. We can stop fretting about our problems and ourselves. We can focus instead on our Savior, expecting Him to provide all we need.

It's a wonderful way to live, but sitting down and keeping our eyes on Jesus isn't always as easy as it sounds.

Problems have a way of screaming to get our attention. It doesn't really matter what they are. Satan will use anything from minor annoyances to major traumas to disrupt our rest and get our eyes off the Lord because that's how he gains access into our lives.

A minister friend of mine was once reminded of that fact in a startling way. He was up early one morning spending time in prayer. Everybody else in the house was still asleep and all was quiet. Suddenly, he heard the sound of somebody on the porch, violently shaking the front door trying to get into the house.

My friend froze. Heart racing, adrenalin pumping, he tensed, ready to fight whoever might come barging in. But nothing happened. For a few seconds, everything went silent. Then he heard the sound again on the other side of the house. It sounded exactly like before, as if someone was rattling a door, trying to break in. But there was no door on that side of the house. A few seconds later, the noise moved again to another place. There was no door there, either.

That's when the Holy Spirit spoke to my friend's heart. *This is no natural intruder,* He said. *What you're hearing is the sound of your enemy looking for a door of access into your life and ministry.*

Although we don't usually hear the sound of it like my friend did, the devil is constantly looking for ways to get into our lives. He's searching for weaknesses in our faith where He can break in and cause trouble. It's sad to say, but many times he gets in without even picking the lock.

I once read an article in our local newspaper that said burglars in our city usually get in through an open window or an unlocked door. Their robberies aren't so much break-ins as they are walk-ins. That's what the devil does to us. He walks in and steals our miracles with ease because we leave the door open for him to do so by taking our eyes off Jesus and focusing on our problems. We give him easy access to our lives by abandoning our place of rest.

It's time we put an end to that. It's time we said, "I'm not playing this game anymore. I'm not letting the devil rob me. I'm locking things down. Satan is not going to gain access to my life by changing my focus. From now on, I'm keeping my attention on God. I'm sitting down by faith."

To be clear, this sort of spiritual sitting isn't just a passive, do-nothing kind of thing. It's a rest of confident expectation. It's having the same attitude the multitude had when they sat down in front of Jesus.

Many of those people had traveled great distances to see Him. They'd heard about the miracles He'd done. They knew that wherever He went He did amazing things. When He told them all to sit down, they got excited. They probably said, "Isn't this awesome? He's about to do something! I'm so glad I came here today. I just knew this was going to be great. I don't know why He's asking us to sit down but He's up to something, that's for sure!"

Those people sat down with expectation.

Do we?

When we go to church, do we expect to receive from God? When we get up every morning, do we have a restful, confident expectation that what God said in His Word is coming to pass for us? Do we live every day expecting Him to move supernaturally on our behalf?

We should, because that kind of expectant faith sets the scene for the miraculous. It gives God an atmosphere He can work in. So sit down, look to Jesus, and expect a miracle.

The Power of Thanksgiving

We find the third principle of limitless living illustrated by what Jesus did next. He took the little dab of food He'd been given—even though it clearly wasn't enough to meet the need—and expressed His gratitude to God. He took the little loaves in His hands and gave thanks.

There's something powerful about having a heart of appreciation for what God has done in our lives and for what He has given us. When we're grateful to our Father for what we already have, it's easy for us to receive more. That's why God instructs us in Psalm 100:4 to "Enter into His gates with thanksgiving, and into His courts with praise. Be thankful to Him, and bless His name."

God doesn't ask us to thank Him and praise Him for His own sake. He's not insecure. He doesn't need our affirmation to feel good about Himself. He wants us to give thanks because thanksgiving helps us enter His presence. It reminds us of His goodness and encourages our faith.

We especially need to express our appreciation to God when we're facing lack. But, you know as well as I do, that's when we're least likely to do it. Instead, we tend to take those opportunities to complain about what we don't have.

Some Christians complain so much they practically become professionals at it. They complain about circumstances and people. They complain about this generation. They complain about the next generation. They complain about the weather and the economy. If they talk about their car, they gripe about what's wrong with it. It's too old. It breaks down. It guzzles gas. It burns oil. Whatever. They never think to be grateful they have a car at all. It doesn't occur to them to say, "Father, thank You for supplying this automobile for me. It's not perfect, but most of the time it gets me where I need to go. I bless this car, Lord, because it's a gift from You. I appreciate it."

That's too bad because thanking God for the car they have could help them build their expectancy for the car they want. Thanksgiving could be a point of contact for their faith. It could open the way for them to thank the Lord not only for what He's already provided, but also for what He's promised in His Word.

An attitude of gratitude in the face of lack paves the way for an outpouring of God's abundance in our lives. If you want evidence of it, just look at what happened that day on the mountainside:

"...Jesus took the loaves, and when He had given thanks He distributed them to the disciples, and the disciples to those sitting down; and likewise

of the fish, as much as they wanted. So when they were filled, He said to His disciples, 'Gather up the fragments that remain, so that nothing is lost.' Therefore they gathered them up, and filled twelve baskets with the fragments of the five barley loaves which were left over by those who had eaten" (John 6:11-13).

This miracle would have been impressive even on a smaller scale. Even if Jesus had only supplied enough for all 20,000 people to have a few bites each, it would have been amazing. But that's not what happened here. Somehow, the loaves and fish kept multiplying until everybody had eaten as much as they wanted with plenty left over!

Notice the Scripture doesn't say the people ate as much as they needed. Need isn't mentioned at all. Jesus didn't have need-meeting on His mind. He set out to satisfy their desire. Give them all they wanted. Some people might have wanted just enough to feel pleasantly full. Others may have wanted to absolutely pig out. (Why not? It was all-you-can-eat *for free*.)

Every person determined the size of their own miracle.

Did you get that? Jesus didn't dictate the size of this miracle. The people did.

God wasn't wringing His hands, worrying that they'd want more then He could provide, either. That's the cool thing about God. He isn't running short of anything. He is well able to "satisfy the desire of every living thing."[55]

---
[55] Psalm 145:16

Do you ever think about how much it takes just to feed all the animals on earth? They all have to eat, you know. Billions of birds and bugs. Oceans full of fish. Everything from African lions to English foxes. We can't even begin to fathom how much stuff has to grow to keep all those critters fed. Yet we don't even think twice about it. We just assume God included their needs when He designed this planetary system. *He's got plenty out there for them,* we think. *They'll be fine.*

Why can't we have the same kind of confidence in His ability to take care of us? Surely a God who can provide for a whole planet full of creatures can satisfy the desires of His own children.

According to the Bible, He not only can...He will. That's the kind of God He is. He's not a cheapskate. He doesn't want us to just skimp by for the rest of our lives. He never meant for us to live continually on the edge of broke, hoping He'll come through for us before we completely run out.

Yes, there may be times like that in our lives. We may have precious and amazing experiences when God supplies an urgent need at the last minute. I remember talking to a believer years ago who told me about such an experience that really blessed him. I'll never forget it. His adventure started with a leading from the Lord to go to South America on a ministry trip.

"But God," he said, "I don't have any money to buy a plane ticket."

That's okay, the Lord answered. *Pack your bags and go to the airport anyway.* So that's what this young man did.

When he arrived at the airport, he got in line to buy his ticket. Three or four people were in front of him. Each time one of them finished their transaction and walked away, this believer said, "Uh...Lord I'm almost to the counter now. This would be a good time for You to provide the money."

Eventually there was just one person in line ahead of him. Concerned he was going to look like a fool, having to ask for a ticket with no money, he prayed again. "Lord, I'd sure like to know what You're going to do here."

About that time, the man in front of him who'd just bought a ticket to South America, turned around and said, "You know, I don't really want to take this trip. Would you like to have this?" Sure enough, the aspiring young missionary took the man's ticket, boarded the plane, and fulfilled the assignment God had given him.

I'll be the first to admit, that's an inspiring testimony. I was happy for the fellow. I believe God does those kinds of things and it thrills and encourages me to hear about it. But I don't want to live that way on a regular basis. I travel every week. I'm buying plane tickets all the time and that's more drama than I want. So my approach is different. I say, "Lord, I want the money in the bank ahead of time."

Abundant provision in advance. That's the way I like to travel.

I was reminded how much I like it a few summers ago when my friend, Jerry Savelle, and I took a motorcycle trip from Los Angeles to Colorado. I charted out the entire route before we ever left town. I knew which highways to take, how much gasoline we'd need, and where the filling stations were. Since we'd be riding through some very desolate country, planning our fuel stops was of paramount importance. That was okay, though, because I had it all handled.

Or so I thought...until, rumbling through a stretch of desert in central Nevada, Jerry pulled his bike up next to mine. "Hey!" he yelled over the noise of the engines, "my fuel light just came on."

Uh, what? How can that be? We're out in the middle of nowhere! (There's a lot of nowhere in Nevada and we were definitely in it.) I looked at my fuel gauge. It showed more than enough gas to make it to Tonopah, the next town which was still many miles away. Jerry's gauge, however, showed less than a gallon left. *Our motorcycles get the same mileage per gallon so why...?*

Uh oh. I glanced over at the little trailer Jerry was pulling behind his bike. I'd failed to figure in the weight of the trailer and the climb in altitude. Obviously, he was using more fuel than I was.

At that moment, our faith kicked in. Jerry and I both started thanking and honoring God in the face of lack. "Oh, Lord Jesus!" we said. "You are the Provider. Thank You for supplying all our needs! Thank You for being the God of abundance!" (It's amazing how much of the Word can flow out of you at a time like that.) We did our best to stay in our place of rest. We also slowed down to 50 miles an hour—call it weakness of faith if you want—to get the best gas mileage possible.

By the time we rolled into the Tonopah filling station, we were really rejoicing over God's faithfulness. When Jerry topped off his tank, we got even happier. It was an absolute miracle his motorcycle made it to the station. His five-gallon gas tank had been sucked so dry that it took 5.13 gallons to fill it back up again. We had no idea where the additional .13 gallons went and we didn't care. We didn't know if Jerry's motorcycle had been running on fumes, pushed along by the Holy Spirit's power, or using supernaturally multiplied fuel. We were just grateful we made it.

Standing next to the dusty gasoline pump in Tonopah, I got a renewed revelation of this important spiritual fact: *It's easier to run on full than it is to run on empty.* If you like the adrenaline rush of running on empty, that's okay with me. You can spend the rest of your life believing God for just enough to escape disaster. You can be a happy running-on-empty person if that's what you enjoy.

But you don't have to do that. It's not what Jesus wants for you. He didn't come to teach you how to live on empty. He came so that you could learn how to live a satisfied life; and a satisfied life is full.

Start the Distribution

Although we usually say it was Jesus who fed the multitudes, that's not really what the Bible teaches. According to John 6:11, "Jesus took the loaves, and when He had given thanks He distributed them to the disciples."

The disciples were the ones who handed out the food. They were the distributors of God's supernatural provision. As they stepped out by faith and began to give away to the thousands the bits of bread and fish Jesus had apportioned to them, those bits kept multiplying until everyone was fed.

That means the miracle actually happened in the hands of the disciples!

It's an astounding thought. But here's one even more amazing. Miracles can happen in our hands too if we'll activate the fourth principle of limitless living and start the distribution.

Every Christian I know dreams of being a distributor. Just like our heavenly Father, we all have a heart to bless people. God made us that way. But we're often hindered in our giving because of a lack mentality. We're afraid that if we give what we have, we'll run out. That's why this story is so encouraging. The more the disciples gave to the multitudes on the mountain, the more they had to give. Instead of not enough, they ended up having too much!

But, then, isn't that what Jesus told us would happen? Didn't He say, "Give, and it will be given to you: good measure, pressed down, shaken together, and running over will it be put into your bosom"?[56]

---

[56] Luke 6:38

Yes, He did! And He's looking right now for people who will believe His words and act on them. He's searching for men and women of faith who will press beyond their own limitations and become distributors for their limitless God. It doesn't matter to Him what their financial status is. It doesn't matter if they only have a little bit. He has the power to take that little bit and make it big.

Jesus has no problem multiplying the provision. But He needs hands He can entrust it to. He needs believers who will be abundance-minded. Believers who can handle great wealth without being ensnared and corrupted by it. Believers who will receive that wealth and distribute it as the Lord directs.

God loves to work miracles in the hands of those kinds of Christians. He'll supply everything they could ever need or want. He'll even set that supply in motion in advance so that it will be there at just the right time. He did it for Jesus all His earthly life. He got the magi moving toward Jerusalem when Jesus was just a baby. They traveled thousands of miles carting camel-loads of wealth as presents for the newborn King. (They didn't show up with three small boxes like you see in nativity scenes. No self-respecting wise man brings one pathetic gift box to a king.)

It took the magi more than two years to complete their journey. Jesus was a toddler by the time they arrived. But they showed up right on time and provided His family with the wealth they needed to go to Egypt and escape Herod's wrath. Think of it! For months and months that money had been on its way. When it arrived, it turned out to be more than enough. The riches of the magi financed Jesus' family for years.

Can God do that kind of thing for you?

Certainly He can and He will if you'll commit to being a distributor. So why not get started? You're already qualified for the job: you're a disciple. You have something (even if it seems small) that you can give, and there are multitudes of people all around you who are hungry for what Jesus can do through you.

Reach out to them. Get the giving going. When you do, God will work miracles through your hands. And there's nothing in the world more satisfying than that.

CHAPTER 7

Leave the Past Behind

"Oh, that You would bless me indeed, and enlarge my territory, that Your hand would be with me, and that You would keep me from evil, that I may not cause pain!"

1 Chronicles 4:10

God is in control.

Without a doubt, it's one of the most spiritual-sounding phrases ever coined. Wildly popular among Christians and non-Christians alike, it's simple to remember and comes in handy when we feel the need to explain the seemingly unexplainable. When somebody asks why bad things happen to good people, instead of shrugging our shoulders and admitting we don't have a clue, we can answer sagely, "Well, you know God is in control and He works in mysterious ways."

People generally appreciate that explanation, not only because it sounds theologically wise but because it relieves us all of a ton of personal responsibility. It's even been set to music from time to time. Several catchy and cool songs have hit the top of the Christian charts by assuring believers that no matter what they do and no matter what happens: God is in control. So, apparently, a lot of people enjoy hearing that.

Too bad it's not true.

Or, then again, maybe it's a good thing it's not true.

Really. Think about it. If God actually is in control of everything that's going on in the world today, He should be fired for doing such a lousy job. It doesn't take omniscience to look around this planet and see that things are in a mess. So if this is all God's fault, and He's the boss of this outfit, we're all in deep trouble.

That seems so obvious you'd think it would cause people to ditch the God-is-in-control perspective. But, for the most part it doesn't. Large portions of the population continue to cling to the idea that God is behind everything that happens in their lives—both good and bad. Never mind what the Bible teaches about Adam, Eve, and the serpent. Never mind the issue of people's free will and their own choices. They'll debate the issue with passion whether it makes sense or not.

I found that out early in my Christian life when I fell into a heated argument about it with an atheist at a bus stop in downtown San Diego. The argument came as a total surprise to me. I certainly didn't go looking for it.

On the contrary, I was out pounding the sun-drenched pavement of southern California that day hoping to win souls, not aggravate them.

Having arrived in town the night before to help with a believers' meeting, I'd spent the morning setting up chairs and getting the auditorium ready for the service. I finished my work early so, grabbing a handful of booklets entitled *Seven Steps to Prayer that Brings Results*, I hit the streets. My plan was to pass out the books (I thought surely people would like to know how to pray and get results since everybody knows how to pray and get nothing) and talk to some folks about Jesus.

Things started out well. The first fellow I talked to was sitting in his car with the window rolled down waiting for his wife who was in one of the stores. I figured if anybody needs to know how to pray it's a guy whose wife is shopping, so I struck up a conversation with him about the Lord. Within a few minutes, the power of God came on the man. He received Jesus as the Lord of his life and got born again. When his wife showed up and found out about it, she dropped her shopping bags and danced right there on the sidewalk. It turned out she'd been praying for him for a long time.

Invigorated by my success, I headed down the street in search of another lost soul and spotted the man sitting on the bench at the bus stop. Having no clue he was an atheist (hostile or otherwise), I smiled at him and held out a booklet. "Hello, sir! I'd like to give you this. It's about prayer that brings results."

Leveling me with a cold-eyed, shark-like stare, he tightened his jaw until the veins popped out on his neck. He didn't reach out to take my pamphlet. He didn't return my smile. "Get away from me," he said. "I don't believe in any of that stuff. I don't believe in prayer and I don't believe in God. If there was a God this world wouldn't be in such terrible shape. There wouldn't be poverty. There wouldn't be disease and crime and death and abuse..." On and on his tirade went.

I wish I could tell you that love just oozed out of me as I endured his rant. I'd like to say that compassion overtook me and I answered with sweetness and light. But I don't want to lie. Maybe today, more than 35 years later, my response would be more mellow. But that day, as I waited with booklet in hand, for shark-man to finish chewing on me, I finally had enough.

"Well, sir," I said when he was done, "you're right that the world is in a mess. But that's not because there is no God. It's because stubborn people like you will not turn your life over to Jesus Christ!"

Not exactly a great evangelistic response. It didn't warm up the situation at all. The atheist, rather than dissolving into tears and giving his heart to the Lord, ratcheted up his volume a couple of decibels, turned to the man sitting next to him (who, no doubt, was desperately hoping the bus would arrive) and said some uncomplimentary things about me and my family heritage.

I might have been a spiritual novice back then, but I had enough sense to know this man wasn't going to want to pray with me. So I took my pamphlet and went looking for greener pastures. Having yielded to the flesh and royally goofed up my attempt to share the Gospel, I walked away as living proof that God isn't always in control.

Five Requests that Can Change Your Life

I don't mind telling that story because everybody, with the exception of Jesus Himself, has done something similar at one time or another. All of us, if we honestly examine our own personal history, have to admit that God hasn't been in control of all our decisions. Nor has He controlled the decisions of those around us.

We were all born into a world of circumstances that were shaped by people's choices, and many of those choices flatly contradicted the will of God. Made out of human ignorance or under demonic pressure, they affected our environment in negative ways. In some cases, even our mothers and fathers, brothers and sisters, friends and teachers may have made choices that hurt us. Choices that pressured us to adopt an identity and take paths God never intended.

But, as we've already seen, we don't have to yield to that pressure. We don't have to let the lousy decisions made by the people around us determine the outcome of our lives. We don't have to live the life everybody else has planned for us. We can live the life that God planned. The Bible assures us we can do it. It says:

"Do not let the world squeeze you into its own mold but let God remold your minds from within so that

127

you can prove in practice that the plan God has for you is good" (Romans 12:2 Phillips).

I've said this before, but it's a point worth repeating: God does have a good plan for your life. No matter how messed up your past may have been. No matter how many mistakes your parents may have made. You are dearly loved by your heavenly Father and He's prepared a wonderful future for you. So don't let other people's choices steal it from you. Don't let the pain of the past choke out your vision for the future.

Instead, take a tip from Jabez. Break the mold that others have set for you. Leave the limits behind and live out your God-inspired dreams.

If Jabez could do it, anybody can. One of my favorite scriptural heroes, he caught my attention many years ago when I was reading the Old Testament. He's only mentioned in two verses but he changed my life by what he chose to believe and how he approached the Lord. He proved to me that it's possible for a person born into circumstances beyond his control to turn his life around through prayer and faith. That an underdog can become an overcomer simply by tapping into the goodness of God.

First Chronicles 4:9-10 tells his story. It says:

"Now Jabez was more honorable than his brothers, and his mother called his name Jabez, saying, 'Because I bore him in pain.' And Jabez called on the God of Israel saying, 'Oh, that You would bless me indeed, and enlarge my territory, that Your hand would be with me, and that You would keep

me from evil, that I may not cause pain!' So God granted him what he requested."

In this one short passage of Scripture, we get a clear sense of the family dynamics at work in Jabez' household. We learn that his brothers were less than honorable and they didn't seek God in any notable way. We learn that Jabez, rather than being swept along with the family tide, chose to go a different direction. We also discover that in a day when fathers were the ones who named their children, Jabez was named by his mother. That means His dad was either dead or totally disconnected from the family. So we know this young man grew up without a father's influence. (Sometimes we think of single parent homes and fatherless households as a modern phenomenon, but it's a problem people have faced for thousands of years. Jabez can testify to it.)

With a house full of other kids, most likely, Jabez' mother didn't have much time for him. Single moms back then, as now, always have their hands full. Even if she'd wanted to help fill the emotional void left in her son's life by his absent father, she didn't have the heart for it. She clearly had issues of her own that got in the way.

It doesn't take a rocket scientist to figure that out. Just look at what she named her boy! *Jabez*, literally translated, means *misery or pain*. This child represented pain to her and she was determined not to let anybody—including him—forget it. She reminded him of it every day of his life. Can you imagine what that must have been like for him?

"Hey, Pain! Time for dinner."

"Hey Misery, make your bed."

"Hurry up, Pain, you'll be late for school."

Wow. That would tend to warp a person. It's a wonder Jabez didn't spend a lifetime on a psychiatrist's couch. Or end up on a talk show as a loser blaming his parents for his failures. With so much going against him, he had every excuse. No dad. Constant criticism from his mom. Wayward brothers. Jabez could have easily given up his dreams and conformed to the pressures around him. He could have said, "Hey, I'm not responsible for how I turned out. I was emotionally abused growing up. I didn't have any good role models."

But he didn't say those things. Instead, he did something nobody else in his family—including his mother—had done. He called on the God of Israel and made five requests. Requests that redefined his life and forever changed his future.

"Oh, that You would bless me indeed, and enlarge my territory . . ."

The first thing Jabez asked for is so simple that most Christians today would be embarrassed to request it. They'd be reluctant to say like he did, "God, I want You to bless me!"

For the most part, believers these days are too sophisticated for that. They've been taught by religion that it's selfish to make such requests of God. In church or other places, they've heard well-meaning preachers say things like "Christianity isn't just a Bless-Me Club. It's not all about you." So they try to keep their prayers on a "higher plane."

Jabez, however, didn't have such religious hang ups. He knew what he wanted and he asked for it.

What gave him such boldness?

Somehow he'd gotten enough insight into God's nature to realize that He wants to do good things for His people. Somehow God revealed to this fatherless little kid named Pain that He is love and love is all about giving. Long before John 3:16 was written, God helped him understand that He isn't looking for ways to get things from people, He's looking for opportunities to give to them. God helped Jabez see that from His perspective, it *is* all about us.

I wish more Christians today could catch hold of that revelation. As God's children we all need to know that blessing us is what floats His boat!

I'm not saying He doesn't enjoy what we give to Him. Certainly He's pleased by our worship and praise. He appreciates our obedience. Our tithes and offerings bring Him pleasure for sure. But He doesn't really need those things. After all, He's Almighty God! What can we do for Him that He can't do for Himself? It's not like He needs us to cook Him a meal or give Him a ride to church. He owns everything so He definitely doesn't need our money. And though He wants us to give Him our hearts and our lives, He only wants it for one reason—so He can show Himself strong on our behalf![57]

---

[57] 2 Chronicles 16:9: "For the eyes of the LORD run to and fro throughout the whole earth, to show Himself strong on behalf of those whose heart is loyal to Him."

God is all about what He can do in us and for us. He's all about what He can give us because He is love. Somehow Jabez got a glimpse of that and it gave him the guts to pray, "God, I want Your blessing in my life!"

The scriptural term *blessing* is a wonderful word. It means to be empowered by God to succeed in every endeavor and triumph continually. God's plan, from the very beginning, was for us to be blessed. The creation account in Genesis makes it abundantly clear. It says that "God created man in His own image...male and female He created them. Then God blessed them, and God said to them, 'Be fruitful and multiply; fill the earth and subdue it; have dominion...'"[58]

Notice, blessing His people was the first thing God did for them. It was at the top of His agenda; and that never changed. When mankind fell into sin and cut themselves off from the blessing, God went to work to restore it. He made covenant with Abraham and, once again, the first thing He said to him was this: "I will bless you...and you shall be a blessing."[59]

After Abraham died, God extended the blessing to his heirs, the children of Israel. Generation after generation, through the Old Covenant, He kept blessing His people until at last Jesus came and opened the way for the whole world to be blessed.[60]

---

[58] Genesis 1:27-28
[59] Genesis 12:2
[60] Galatians 3:13-14: Christ has redeemed us from the curse of the law, having become a curse for us (for it is written, "Cursed is everyone who hangs on a tree"), that the blessing of Abraham might come upon the Gentiles in Christ Jesus, that we might receive the promise of the Spirit through faith.

Because the Bible refers to the concept of *blessing* in one form or another literally hundreds of times, it's obvious that blessing us is a big deal to God. So, it ought to be a big deal to us too. We should study everything the Bible has to say about it. We need to find out from the Scriptures everything God's blessing includes—not only so that we can take full advantage of it in our own lives, but so that we can be a blessing to others. (You can't bless others very much if you're not blessed yourself.)

If you'll study what God's Word says about the subject, you'll get free from a lot of religious bondage. You'll see it confirms again and again that God's blessings are not just spiritual, they're material as well. Jabez, for instance, specifically asked God to bless him by prospering him financially. "Enlarge my territory!" he said. Some translations put it this way: *Give me more land!* In Jabez' day, land equaled wealth and influence. So, in essence, he was saying, "God, enlarge my financial situation. Increase my capacity to influence people for the kingdom of God."

Anybody who doesn't believe God is interested in increasing His people financially hasn't read the Bible. It absolutely settles the issue. Again and again it says things like this:

- "The LORD will command the blessing on you in your storehouses [a.k.a. checking accounts, savings accounts, and investment portfolios] and in all to which you set your hand" (Deuteronomy 28:8).

- "And the LORD will grant you plenty of goods, in the fruit of your body, in the increase of your

133

livestock, and in the produce of your ground" (verse 11).

- "The blessing of the LORD makes one rich, and He adds no sorrow with it" (Proverbs 10:22).

- "Blessed is the man who fears the LORD, who delights greatly in His commandments...Wealth and riches will be in his house, and his righteousness endures forever" (Psalm 112:1,3).

- "For you know the grace of our Lord Jesus Christ, that though He was rich, yet for your sakes He became poor, that you through His poverty might become rich" (2 Corinthians 8:9).

- "And God is able to make all grace abound toward you, that you, always having all sufficiency in all things, may have an abundance for every good work" (2 Corinthians 9:8).

Jabez didn't have all those verses to read like we do. Yet somehow he had faith enough to believe that God would increase his wealth. Somehow he realized that his desire to be blessed and enlarged financially didn't offend God. In fact, it honored Him. So, instead of apologizing for it, he turned it into a prayer that pushed back the limits of his life.

Asking for Guidance and Protection

The next request Jabez made of God was this one: *Let Your hand be with me.* We've already proven that Jabez wasn't bound up by a bunch of religious nonsense. So we know that he wasn't asking God just to be present wherever he went. Although people often pray that kind of thing, it's a waste of breath.

God is everywhere. Where can we go that He's not? As the psalmist says, "...where can I flee from Your presence? If I ascend into heaven, You are there; if I make my bed in hell, behold, You are there."[61] Since it's pointless to pray, "God be with me," and Jabez wasn't a pointless pray-er, obviously he must have had something else in mind.

What was it?

He wanted God's direction in his life. He wanted God to lead him so he'd know what to do and where to go.

He was saying, like David did in Psalm 123, "...as the eyes of servants look to the hand of their masters, as the eyes of a maid to the hand of her mistress, so our eyes look to the LORD our God."[62] When a servant is attending the needs of the guests at his master's dinner party, the master doesn't want to interrupt his guests' conversations by calling out commands to the servant. So he signals silently with his hand to let him know what to do. By watching the master's hand, the servant knows which dishes need to be cleared away and when it's time to bring out the next course.

That's the kind of thing Jabez had in mind when asked for God's hand to be with him. As an Israelite, he'd heard the stories about the many times God had brought

---

[61] Psalm 139:7-8
[62] Verse 2

deliverance to his people. He'd been told how God directed them and empowered them with His hand to overcome overwhelming odds. Jabez knew what it was like to face those kinds of odds. The circumstantial deck was definitely stacked against him.

He knew that if he played the hand other people's choices had dealt him, he'd end up making the same mistakes his family members had made. But he wanted to be delivered from that kind of life. So he looked to God for direction. He asked the Almighty One who so many times had given the underdog nation of Israel a hand up and brought them out on top, to do the same for him. He said, "Show me how to live my life Your way so that I can come out a winner."

That prayer resonates with all of us, doesn't it? Every true child of God has a heartfelt desire to be led and directed by their heavenly Father. "Lord, I want to know what you want me to do!" we say. "I want Your hand to guide me where You want me to go. I want You to show me the best way to approach the situations in my life."

That's a scriptural prayer. And God will answer it for us just as surely as he answered it for Jabez.

He'll also do for us the next thing Jabez asked. "Keep me from evil!" Jesus confirmed that's God's will for us in the prayer recorded in John 17 when He prayed for us, as His disciples, and said, "Father...

"I'm saying these things...so my people can experience my joy completed in them. I gave them your

word; the godless world hated them because of it, because they didn't join in the world's ways, just as I didn't join the world's ways. I'm not asking that you take them out of the world but that you guard them from the Evil One" (verses 13-15 The Message).

As born again believers, we have a right to be kept from evil because we've been bought and paid for by the blood of Jesus. We belong to God. Satan has no right to us or to anything that's ours. He has no right to our life, our health, our family, our future, our thinking, or our money. But here's what we must remember: the devil is a thief. He's a lawbreaker. He will trespass on God's property if we let him.

But, praise God, we don't have to let him!

We can stand on God's Word and believe that we are protected. We can be confident that because of what Jesus prayed for us and what He did for us in His death and resurrection, God is on our side. The Evil One is defeated and no weapon formed against us shall prosper.[63]

In essence, through Jesus, God has done for us what He did for Job. He put a hedge around him, around his household, and around all that he had on every side so that Satan couldn't touch him.[64] Of course, to enjoy the

---

[63] Isaiah 54:17: "No weapon formed against you shall prosper, And every tongue which rises against you in judgment You shall condemn. This is the heritage of the servants of the LORD, And their righteousness is from Me," says the LORD.
[64] Job 1:10

safety of that hedge, Job had to stay inside it and so do we. We can't dance with the devil in some areas of our lives and still enjoy divine protection. We can't compromise and think we're going to get the benefits of obedience when we're living in disobedience.

We have to stay close to God and obey His commands. But that's okay because those commands are not irksome, hard, or oppressive. They're delightfully simple. The Bible sums them up this way: put your faith in Jesus and walk in love.[65] When we do those things (and God will empower us by His grace to do them) we can rest assured that our hedge is intact. We can live like Jabez did, confident that "The God-begotten are also the God-protected. The Evil One can't lay a hand on them" (1 John 5:18, The Message).

Reinvent My Life!

Every request Jabez made was amazing. Everything he asked God to do indicated a high level of faith and a remarkable degree of revelation. But the last phrase of his petition topped them all. He ended his prayer by saying, in essence, "God, reinvent my life so that I don't cause pain!" With those words, Jabez opened the door for God to give him a whole new identity.

It's only by God's mercy that Jabez knew such a thing was possible. It's a miracle he could even imagine it. After all, his entire life he'd been defined by his mother, his brothers, and everyone who knew him as a person who

---

[65] 1 John 3:23: And this is His commandment: that we should believe on the name of His Son Jesus Christ and love one another, as He gave us commandment.

brings pain. He heard that definition of himself every time someone called his name. For him to be a blessing to anybody, he'd need an extreme identity makeover.

A lot of believers today are in the same situation. Their mothers may not have literally named them Pain, but they were born into circumstances just as miserable. Some were abused as children, mistreated so badly that it absolutely wrecked their ability to handle life. It's all they can do just to get up every morning and face another day. Even though they're saved and they know Jesus, they're still living out the script written for them by other people's choices. Voices from their past are programming their future. "You're never going to make it. Nobody in your family has ever amounted to anything and you won't either. Your grandfather was a failure; your dad was a failure; and you'll be a failure too."

All of us have been told such things at one time or another. As kids, we tried to act like they didn't bother us. We learned to say, "Sticks and stones can break my bones but words will never hurt me." It sounded like a cool response when we were in grade school. It gave us something to say to bullies on the playground. But as the years passed we realized it isn't true.

People's words are powerful. They lodge in our memories. They pierce our hearts. Our childhood chant was wrong. Just like sticks and stones, words really can hurt us.

I'm sure Jabez understood that better than most. But he also understood this: God can undo the damage. He can speak words to us and about us that are powerful enough to obliterate all the negative things other people have said.

God's words are more than just information. They're spirit and life.[66] When we believe them and speak them over ourselves, they supersede everything else that's been said about us. They enable us to see ourselves so completely in the light of God's love that the opinions of others can no longer cast a shadow over our lives. They set us so free that we can respond the same way Jesus did to those who criticize and put us down. We can say (and really mean it), "Your approval or disapproval means nothing to me."[67]

I love that statement! When Jesus said it He was talking to the religious leaders who were trying to pass judgment on Him. They were trying to box Him in with their man-made ideas of what He should be and say and do. They were defining Him according to their own worldly, wrong-headed perspective; calling Him a madman; and accusing Him of being in league with the devil.

Most of us would get our feelings hurt if people talked about us that way. We'd start feeling insecure and inadequate. We'd start wondering if we really are as bad as people say. But not Jesus. He just shrugged off those negative words. He couldn't care less about what people thought of Him or said about Him. He knew what God said about Him and that knowledge set Him free.

"Yeah, but Dennis, that was *Jesus!*"

---

[66] John 6:63: "It is the Spirit who gives life; the flesh profits nothing. The words that I speak to you are spirit, and they are life."
[67] John 5:41 NLT

I know, but we can follow His example. We can lay hold of that kind of freedom, too. That's what Jabez did. He came to the conclusion that he didn't have to be what everybody else said he was. He didn't have to be a person who lives in misery and brings pain for the rest of his life. Jabez decided he could let God redefine him. And, according to the Bible, that's exactly what God did. He "granted him what he requested."

He'll do the same for us. But first we have to open the door for Him to do it. At some point we must put our faith in Him and stop allowing other people's choices to determine our destiny. We must draw the line in the sand and say, "I'm not living like this anymore! I refuse to spend the rest of my life under the shadow of other people's words and opinions. I'm throwing out the trash that was dumped on me in the past and I'm taking on my true, God-given identity."

As Christians, we often talk about how much we want to be like Jesus. Well, this is how we get to be like Him. We let Him and His Word redefine us. Instead of surrendering to the circumstances we were born into, instead of just rolling over, playing the victim and saying, "Well, you know, God is in control. I guess there's just nothing I can do to change this," we can rise up and say:

This is a new day. I'm a new person in Christ Jesus. Old things are gone and all things have become new. I'm not a product of this messed up world any more. My circumstances can't limit me. Although I've had some trouble in my life, it hasn't been God's fault. He didn't cause it. But He will deliver me from it. He will do for me everything He did for Jabez. He'll bless me, enlarge me, guide me, protect me, and make me a blessing to others. The negative words in my past no longer have the power to contain or control me. Jesus has made me free.

Let God Keep the Books

"I tell you, love your enemies. Help and give without expecting a return. You'll never—I promise—regret it. Live out this God-created identity the way our Father lives toward us, generously and graciously, even when we're at our worst...Don't pick on people, jump on their failures, criticize their faults—unless, of course, you want the same treatment. Don't condemn those who are down; that hardness can be a boomerang. Be easy on people; you'll find life a lot easier. Give away your life; you'll find life given back, but not merely given back—given back with bonus and blessing. Giving, not getting, is the way. Generosity begets generosity."

Luke 6:35-38 The Message

I learned early in my Christian life that my walk with Jesus doesn't depend on anybody else. My satisfaction, my victory, my joy doesn't come from what people around me do or don't do. Although I love the fellowship of other believers and I'm grateful to be a part of the family of God, I can't allow myself to look to others as the source of my spiritual strength and identity. I can't afford to crumble when they don't say nice things about me or pat me on the back.

I have to stand up for who I am in Christ no matter what everybody else is doing and saying because, like it or not, people will fail me. So if I can't stand alone in Christ, I can't stand at all.

The prayer we studied in Chapter 7 indicates Jabez understood that. He demonstrated it not only by what he requested of God, but also by what he didn't. Think about it. Jabez never mentioned anything in his prayer about how his mother or his brothers behaved. He didn't point to their shabby treatment and say, "Lord, You need to punish them! You need to show them where they're wrong and make them apologize to me!"

Nope. Jabez never even brought them up. Apparently he understood that their deeds and misdeeds weren't any of his business.

I don't know when Jabez got that revelation but I know when I did. It was in 1973. I was in youth ministry at a thriving church in Los Angeles serving under Senior Pastor Herb Ezell. God knows I love Pastor Ezell and I'll be forever grateful for the investment he made in my life, but he wasn't the easiest person to work for. He wasn't big on appreciation and affirmation. He told me straight up one time, "Dennis, the world is a tough place and ministry is a lot of hard work. If you're doing it for a pat on the back, you're in the wrong place. You'll spend most of your life being unappreciated so you might as well get used to it now."

One day during my tenure at Pastor Ezell's church, I was in my office attempting to pray over the youth ministry and I kept being distracted by a rumbling noise coming from the office of the associate pastor across the hall. I'd heard the noise before and ignored it. But on this particular day I decided I couldn't take it anymore. I had to see for myself what was going on over there. So I tiptoed over to the associate pastor's office and leaned in far enough to see him with his head on the desk, sound asleep.

Seized with indignation, I quickly tallied up the injustices involved. Number one: here I am working hard, praying fervently over the work of the Lord while this so-called minister is sawing logs in the middle of the day. Number two: as associate pastor, he's higher on the ladder of church authority than I am. Number three: his salary is bigger than mine!

"There's something majorly wrong with this and I'm not going to put up with it!" I fumed. Marching down to the pastor's office, I knocked on the door of the reception area where his secretary, Debbie, stood guard. *Whoosh.* Debbie slid open the little window above her desk and peered out at me. "Hello, Dennis," she said, "what can I do for you?"

"I need to see Pastor Ezell," I huffed.

"Do you have an appointment?"

"Debbie, you keep the appointment book. You know I don't have an appointment. But I need to see Pastor Ezell and I need to see him right now!"

"Well...wait just a moment and I'll ask him if he's available." *Whoosh.* She slid the window closed again.

I waited, steaming, my flesh preparing its self-righteous rant. *Whoosh.* The window opened again. "The Pastor will see you now," Debbie informed me.

Sitting across the desk from Pastor Ezell, I laid out my case against the associate pastor. I regurgitated my list of grievances, pointing out my diligence vs. his laziness, my praying vs. his sleeping, and the unfairness of it all. (I thought it best not to mention outright the difference in our salaries.)

Pastor Ezell rocked his chair back in silence when I finished, gazing up at the ceiling with a disgustingly wise expression on his face. Finally, in his own good time, he said, "Dennis, let me ask you a question. Who do you work for?"

Pinpricks of sweat threatened to break out on my forehead as I tried to come up with an equally wise answer. *Oh man, I gotta get this right!*

"I'm working for God," I blurted.

Pastor Ezell leaned forward and leveled a withering gaze at me across the desk. "Well, Dennis, He keeps the books..." Long pause. "Anything else?"

"Uh, no sir. I don't think so."

Slinking back to my office, I prayed for the associate pastor to have sweet dreams. *I don't care what you do, my friend. Sleep well, if you want,* I thought. *God keeps the books.*

Pastor Ezell is in heaven now but those words still ring in my ears. They changed my life. I'll remember until the day I die—and afterward too because Pastor Herb Ezell will be reminding me for all eternity—that God keeps the books. In the end, I'm going to reap what I sow. What I do from my heart will generate results in my own life.

It doesn't matter what everybody else is doing. It doesn't matter what it looks like they're getting away with. Other people's behavior is none of my business. My business is to do what God has called me to do because when I stand before Jesus one day, He's not going to talk to me about anybody else. He's going to talk to me about me. He's either going to look at me with satisfaction and say, "Well done, good and faithful servant!" or He's going to look at me with disappointment and say, "Well...?"

If I want to hear the *well done!* I can't afford to waste time worrying about the seeming inequities and injustices around me. I have to leave those things to God, trusting Him to keep the books. I have to live in confidence that He is just and if I live by faith in His justice He'll see to it that things turn out right for me. If I put my trust in Jesus, He'll treat me as if I'd never sinned and reward me richly for serving Him out of the integrity of my heart.

Actually, the treating-me-as-if-I'd-never-sinned part of that arrangement isn't so much justice as it is mercy because, behaviorally, I don't deserve to be treated that way. Neither do you. We've all sinned...a lot! But that's the great thing about God's justice: it always begins (and ends) with His mercy. His first act of bookkeeping wipes out the sin debt we owe and credits us with His own record of perfection.

What a great deal! We could never pay off our debt or earn a sinless status with our good works. No matter how hard we tried, we'd always come up short. But God, in His kindness, sent Jesus to balance the books, to take the riches of His own righteousness and give it to us as a gift that becomes ours the moment we believe. Romans 4:5-8 in the New Living Translation says it this way:

> *"[God's] people are declared righteous because of their faith, not because of their work. King David spoke of this, describing the happiness of an unde-serving sinner who is declared to be righteous: 'Oh, what joy for those whose disobedience is forgiven, whose sins are put out of sight. Yes, what joy for those whose sin is no longer counted against them by the Lord.'"*

The idea of God keeping the books would be scary if God was still counting our sin against us. But that's not His role in our lives. He's not looking to see what we're doing wrong so that He can punish us. He's keeping the books on our faith in Him. He's watching to see how we follow Him and what we're believing for. He's looking for avenues through which He can release blessing to us.

For those of us who've been justified by the blood of Jesus, God's bookkeeping is good news because He is always looking to increase us and multiply His goodness in our lives.

Always.

Learning the Lesson of Absalom and Ahithophel

"But Dennis," you might say, "does that mean the people who've done me wrong aren't going to have to pay for it? Are they going to get a pass just because they put their faith in God? It's not fair for them to go free when I'm still hurting!"

Ah, that's the problem, isn't it?

God's forgiving, merciful form of justice seems very fair when it applies to us. But when it applies to others— particularly those who hurt us—we sometimes resent it. We try to get around it by setting ourselves up as judges and rendering our own verdict about whether or not the guilty ones have truly repented. We decide for ourselves whether or not they deserve to be pardoned for their transgressions against us.

Jesus clearly told us not to do that. "Judge not, that you be not judged,"[68] He warned. But when we're feeling the sting of somebody else's wrongdoing, we're often sorely tempted to disobey Him.

What can we do in those instances to help keep us on track? How can we encourage ourselves to keep our self-righteous flesh out of the judgment seat that belongs to Christ alone?

---

[68] Matthew 7:1

Here's an idea. We can remind ourselves of Absalom and Ahithophel, two people whose examples we do not want to follow. Their stories serve as a sobering lesson about what can happen when we, as God's people, take justice into our own hands. Their mistakes practically scream at us from the pages of Scripture, *"Do not pass this way!"*

Absalom and Ahithophel occupy a place in one the most pivotal times in Old Testament history—the reign of King David. Absalom, David's son, and Ahithophel, David's closest advisor, both played major roles in the life of the man described in the Bible as: *a man after God's own heart; the anointed of the God of Jacob; and the sweet psalmist of Israel.*[69] It sounds like an honor, doesn't it? Who wouldn't want to be closely associated with a man like that?

Absalom and Ahitophel, that's who. They thought less highly of David than God did. They had good reasons for it, too. They both felt he'd done them great harm. And they carried a serious grudge against him because of it.

The reason for Ahithophel's grudge could be summed up in one word: Bathsheba. You've probably heard the name. Most people these days have. Even though she lived thousands of years ago, almost everybody who owns a Bible knows what happened between her and David. They know about the sin involved and the grief that resulted.

What most people don't know, however, is this: Ahithophel was Bathsheba's grandfather. He and his

---

[69] 1 Samuel 13:14; 2 Samuel 23:1

family felt the repercussions of the infamous events from 2 Samuel 11 far more deeply than most. They are recounted this way:

> *"It happened in the spring of the year, at the time when kings go out to battle, that David sent Joab and his servants with him, and all Israel; and they destroyed the people of Ammon and besieged Rabbah. But David remained at Jerusalem. Then it happened one evening that David arose from his bed and walked on the roof of the king's house. And from the roof he saw a woman bathing, and the woman was very beautiful to behold. So David sent and inquired about the woman. And someone said, "Is this not Bathsheba, the daughter of Eliam, the wife of Uriah the Hittite?" Then David sent messengers, and took her; and she came to him, and he lay with her" (verses 1-4).*

If you've heard the story, you know what happened next. Bathsheba got pregnant. David, panic-stricken and attempting to hide his adultery, called her husband, Uriah, home from the battlefield. He assumed Uriah would take the opportunity for a conjugal visit with his wife and, thus, it would appear that her conception had taken place in an appropriate and godly way. (What a plan! What a man of God!)

Uriah, however, turned out to have more integrity than David anticipated. Refusing the pleasure of his wife's company, he slept at the king's door with the servants. When David asked him why he did it, he said, "The Ark and the armies of Israel and Judah are living in tents, and Joab and his officers are camping in the open fields. How could I go home to wine and dine and sleep with my wife? I swear that I will never be guilty of acting like that" (v. 11 NLT).

David spent the next few days plying Uriah with alcohol thinking that if he got a little drunk, he'd change his mind. But it didn't make any difference. Tipsy or not, Uriah still insisted on sleeping outside.

With his original plan foiled, David came up with a more sinister solution. He wrote a letter to Joab, the commander of his army, sealed it with the king's seal and gave it to Uriah to deliver.

> *"The letter instructed Joab, 'Station Uriah on the front lines where the battle is fiercest. Then pull back so that he will be killed.' So Joab assigned Uriah to a spot close to the city wall where he knew the enemy's strongest men were fighting. And Uriah was killed along with several other Israelite soldiers" (verses 15-17 NLT).*

These days we think Hollywood has the corner on scandals, but there isn't a story in the world more scandalous than this one in the life of David. It includes adultery, betrayal of a best friend (David knew full well that Bathsheba was Ahithophel's granddaughter), lies, scheming, and murder. For a while, David thought the story would end all right. He thought he'd be able to cover up his sin. He married Bathsheba and figured he could just sweep the whole mess under the rug.

Then one day, he heard a knock on the door. It seemed Nathan, the prophet of God, had stopped by for a visit.

He didn't tell David at first why he'd come. He simply launched into a story about two men—one rich and one poor—who lived in a certain town. "The rich man owned many sheep and cattle," Nathan said. "The poor man owned nothing but a little lamb he had worked hard to buy. He raised that little lamb, and it grew up with his children. It ate from the man's own plate and drank from his cup. He cuddled it in his arms like a baby daughter."

It was a peculiar way to start a conversation, for sure. But David knew Old Testament prophets often behaved in strange ways. So he listened politely as Nathan wrapped up his tale with a stunner of an ending. "One day a guest arrived at the home of the rich man. But instead of killing a lamb from his own flocks for food, he took the poor man's lamb and killed it and served it to his guest."

Aghast at the heartbreaking turn the story had taken, David erupted in fury. "As surely as the LORD lives," he vowed, "any man who would do such a thing deserves to die! He must repay four lambs to the poor man for the one he stole and for having no pity."

Nathan's eyes must have flashed with divine anger as he drove his reply like a dagger into David's heart. "You are that man!" he said. Then he proceeded to deliver a scorching rebuke from God, spelling out all the grotesque sins David had committed against Bathsheba and Uriah.

The full horror of the punishment David faced at that moment sometimes escapes us as New Testament believers. We don't think about the fact that under Old Testament law there was no atonement for the kinds of sin David had committed. There was no provision made for him to be forgiven. The law simply demanded that, as an adulterer and murderer, he be taken outside the camp of Israel and stoned to death by the elders of the land.

Death was the only future David could legally claim and he knew it.

But here's the amazing thing about him. He understood the merciful nature of God in a way that few others did at that point in history. Although he had an awesome respect for God's holiness and he realized that sin was nothing to fool around with, he also knew that God didn't want to kill anybody for their sin. God wanted to redeem them. He wanted to forgive them.

Even though there was no Old Covenant sacrifice or offering that would cover what David had done, he knew the desire of God's heart was to show him mercy. So by the time Nathan was finished with his excruciating litany of David's sins, David was thoroughly repentant and calling out for forgiveness. Psalm 51 records his prayer:

"Have mercy upon me, O God, according to Your lovingkindness; according to the multitude of Your tender mercies, blot out my transgressions. Wash me thoroughly from my iniquity, and cleanse me from my sin. For I acknowledge my transgressions, and my sin is always before me. Against You, You only, have I sinned, and done this evil in Your sight; that You may be found just when You speak, and blameless when You judge. Behold, I was brought forth in iniquity, and in sin my mother conceived me. Behold, You desire truth in the inward parts, and in the hidden part You will make me to know

wisdom. Purge me with hyssop, and I shall be clean; wash me, and I shall be whiter than snow" *(verses 1-7).*

As if in answer to that prayer, Nathan declared, "... the LORD has forgiven you, and you won't die for this sin."[70]

Somehow that day David reached out by faith and laid hold of the sin-canceling power of the New Covenant. His transgressions were removed from him as far as the east is from the west. God's mercy triumphed over judgment,[71] David's life was spared, and he went on to be the greatest king Israel has ever known.

Good for David.

Not so good, however, for Ahithophel.

God's merciful justice didn't satisfy him. He spent the rest of his life resenting how David had violated his beautiful granddaughter and wounded his family. While pretending to be David's most faithful friend, he nurtured seeds of resentment in his heart year after year. And as they always do, those seeds eventually sprouted and bore the bitter fruit of revenge.

From Getting Mad to Getting Even

The opportunity arose when Ahithophel found a co-conspirator in David's son, Absalom, who had cultivated quite a bitter garden of his own. His resentment stemmed

---

[70] 2 Samuel 12:1-13 NLT
[71] James 2:13

from his father's failure to deal with a shameful, family tragedy: the rape of Absalom's sister, Tamar, by his half-brother, Amnon.

Although the rape itself was an awful thing, Tamar's honor could have been restored under Old Covenant law if Amnon had married her. But he refused. Instead, after raping her, he rejected her. He left her a desolate, dishonored, ruined woman. Taking refuge in Absalom's house, living on his kindness, Tamar waited on David to do the right thing. To fulfill his responsibility as father and king. To deal justly with Amnon and demand recompense for Tamar.

But it never happened. When David got word of the situation, he got angry but he never did anything. Never said a word about it. He simply ignored the situation and went on with his life.

Absalom, who loved Tamar dearly, saw his father's negligence as unforgivable. David had not only abandoned his daughter in her time of greatest need, he'd proven himself a coward, unfit to be king. So Absalom resolved to remedy the situation. Convinced that Israel deserved a better, more honorable leader, he plotted his own form of justice. He determined in his heart that one day he would remove his father from the throne of Israel and take his place.

Ahithophel, of course, enthusiastically approved of that plan. Employing the expertise he'd gained through years of service in David's government, he went to work with Absalom designing the details of a deadly coup.

What they did was wrong, no question about it. Yet most of us can admit we'd be tempted to do the same thing if we were in their shoes. Seriously. How would we reconcile the fact that God condemns adultery, rape, murder, and the like, with the fact that our leader—a man supposedly anointed and called of God—had committed those very crimes against our loved ones and gone unpunished?

Although to a lesser degree, all of us face circumstances like that at one time or another. We all experience hurt and see injustices seemingly ignored. In fact, the longer we live, the more opportunities we have to feel violated, take offense, and become seedbeds of bitterness. How are we supposed to respond in those situations? Are we supposed to just look the other way? Pretend that everything is okay?

No, not at all.

We have to deal with those things before God. We have to go to Him for help, reassurance, and a right perspective. We have to remind ourselves that He's keeping the books. Ahithophel and Absalom didn't do that. They chose to keep the books—and settle the accounts—themselves. They passed judgment on David and then tried to execute the punishment they decided he deserved. They devised a clever scheme that would have worked if it hadn't been for the divinely ordained interference of one man: a true friend of David's named Hushai.

Thank heaven for Hushai! A man who'd seen David's failures and yet refused to be swayed by them, he remained loyal to his God-anointed king. He stuck with

David even after the conspirators drove him out of Jerusalem and sent him running for his life. According to the Bible, Hushai showed up on the first miserable day of David's exile when he went up to the Mount of Olives:

> *"...And wept as he went up; and he had his head covered and went barefoot. And all the people who were with him covered their heads and went up, weeping as they went up. Then someone told David, saying, 'Ahithophel is among the conspirators with Absalom.' And David said, 'O LORD, I pray, turn the counsel of Ahithophel into foolishness!'"*

Notice that right in the middle of this disastrous situation David cried out to God in prayer. (Good call.) In his prayer, he made a very specific request. He asked God to disrupt Ahithophel's counsel. Why was that so important to David? Because Ahithophel had been so close to him for so long that he understood how David thought. He had the wisdom to bring him down. David knew that if Absalom followed Ahithophel's counsel, the rebellion would succeed and David would not only lose his throne, he would lose his life.

This was a critical moment. David desperately needed a quick answer to his prayer. Sure enough, he got it. Right after he said, "Amen,"

> *"...When David had come to the top of the mountain, where he worshiped God; there was Hushai the Archite coming to meet him with his robe torn and dust on his head. David said to him, 'If you go on with me, then you will become a burden to me. But if you return to the city, and say to Absalom,*

"I will be your servant, O king; as I was your father's servant previously, so I will now also be your servant," then you may defeat the counsel of Ahithophel for me"' (2 Samuel 15:30-34).

The scheme worked perfectly. Hushai went back to Jerusalem and convinced David's enemies he was on their side. Once in the inner circle, he acted as a spy and a saboteur. When Ahithophel wisely advised Absalom to pursue David immediately, Hushai countered with another suggestion. He said, "The advice that Ahithophel has given is not good at this time." Then he told Absalom it would be better to wait awhile, to gather an army and go after David when they were better prepared.

Absalom agreed with Hushai and decided to follow his counsel. Ahithophel, knowing the result would be disastrous and end in Absalom's defeat, "saddled a donkey, and arose and went home to his house, to his city. Then he put his household in order, and hanged himself, and died; and he was buried in his father's tomb" (2 Samuel 17:14,23).

Ahithophel ended his life in despondence and despair. Everything he'd lived for—his reputation, his place of honor in Israel, the revenge he'd planned for so many years—had collapsed in the blink of an eye. He had no future left and he knew it. So he took his own life. He died in misery, hating the man God had called him to serve, robbed of his divine destiny, all because he refused to let go of an injustice he'd suffered.

Absalom didn't fare any better. When he led his army out against David's, his forces were slaughtered. Riding on a mule, trying to escape the carnage, Absalom caught his hair—a long, beautiful mane he'd always been quite proud of—in the branches of a tree. He dangled there helpless for a while, still seething with hatred for his father and blaming him for all that had happened, until the commander of David's army arrived and thrust him through with not one, but three spears.

Like Ahithophel, Absalom died in bitterness and anger. He let the devil deprive him of his royal place in history and a potentially glorious future. All because he refused to forgive his father's failures. All because he wouldn't trust God to keep the books.

Don't Let It Happen to You

I come across Christians all the time who are making the same mistake. They've been violated at some point and they refuse to put it behind them. They've let bitterness take root in them and it controls them. It drives them to demand their own kind of justice. It stops them from walking in the kind of joy God offers. I've met believers who've put their whole life on hold because they're waiting for the person who hurt them to pay the price for it. They're waiting for the fairness scales to be balanced. They may even be looking for ways to balance those scales themselves.

Following the path of Absalom and Ahithophel, they're heading toward a tragic end.

Please understand, I'm not criticizing those believers or suggesting they should never stand up for themselves. I'm not saying Christians must all live like doormats.

That we must let people abuse us any way they want while we just keep our mouths shut and take it. No, let me be absolutely clear on this point. God hasn't called us to be voluntary victims.

Walking in love and forgiveness doesn't require us to endure every kind of foul treatment people dish out to us without saying a word to them about it. That's not the point of this story. Absalom and Ahithophel didn't have to sit by in silence while David sinned against them and their loved ones. They could have gone to him and confronted him. They could have let him know how wrong he was and how they felt about it. They could have given him an opportunity to repent.

That's what God did. He sent Nathan to give David one of the most soul-convicting lectures in Scripture. If David hadn't responded with repentance, he would have paid for his sins with his life. God would have swiftly and severely settled the score.

Think about how differently things could have turned out for Absalom and Ahithophel if they'd followed God's pattern. Think what could have happened if they'd brought their grievances to David and he'd wept and pled for their forgiveness. They could have rallied around him and turned the whole situation around. They could have gone on to fulfill key roles in the greatest royal dynasty the world has ever seen. They could have shared kinship, friendship, and triumphs with Israel's greatest king.

"Yeah, but what if they'd confronted David and he didn't repent?"

They could have simply trusted God to deal with the situation. Refusing to let past hurts define them, they could have put the scales of justice in His hands where they belong and gotten back to the business of obeying God in their own lives. I guarantee you, sooner or later God would have made things right for them.

If you need proof, just look at how things turned out for David.

Essentially, he ended up facing the same kind of betrayal from Absalom and Ahithophel that he'd originally dealt to them. But David handled it in a completely different way. He didn't get mad and start plotting his own revenge. He didn't just pretend nothing had happened, either. He didn't try to keep a stiff upper lip and (as some people say) "just get over it."

No, he laid the whole situation out before God in prayer. He got completely honest about what he thought and how he felt. He didn't cover anything up. He didn't try to present the situation in a positive light but, describing to God the horror of it in no uncertain terms, he said:

"Listen to my prayer, O God. Do not ignore my cry for help! Please listen and answer me, for I am overwhelmed by my troubles. My enemies shout at me, making loud and wicked threats. They bring trouble on me, hunting me down in their anger. My heart is in anguish. The terror of death overpowers me. Fear and trembling overwhelm me. I can't stop shaking. Oh, how I wish I had wings like a dove; then I would fly away and rest! I would fly far away to the quiet of the wilderness...How quickly I would

escape—far away from this wild storm of hatred" *(Psalm 55:1-8 NLT).*

Why did David feel the need to recite to God all those gory details? Didn't he realize that God already knew everything that was going on?

Certainly he realized it. David wasn't trying to give God information He might not have. He was praying those things for his own sake. He needed to say them. He needed the comfort that always came when he poured out his troubles to the only One in the universe who could do anything about them—his heavenly Father.

When we're hurting, we as New Testament believers often need that same kind of comfort. We need to stop playing religious games and reciting pretty prayers and get real with God. We need to say, "Father, I just need to tell you what's happened, how bad it stinks, and exactly how I feel about it."

To some people such prayers might sound like shocking stuff, but apparently not to David. He was just getting started. Just look at what he prayed next!

"Destroy them, Lord, and confuse their speech, for I see violence and strife in the city. Its walls are patrolled day and night against invaders, but the real danger is wickedness within the city.

"Murder and robbery are everywhere there; threats and cheating are rampant in the streets. It is not an enemy who taunts me—I could bear that. It is not my foes who so arrogantly insult me—I could have hidden from them. Instead, it is [Ahithophel]—my

equal, my companion and close friend. What good
fellowship we enjoyed as we walked together to
the house of God. Let death seize my enemies by
surprise; let the grave swallow them alive, for evil
makes its home within them" (verses 9-15 NLT).

Don't get me wrong here. I'm not suggesting you
follow this pattern exactly. Nowhere in the New Testament are we taught to pray for people to be killed and
destroyed just because they've mistreated us. On the
contrary, we're taught to pray like Jesus did, "Father,
forgive them for they know not what they do." But let's be
honest. Sometimes we can't do that right away. When our
wounded emotions are still throbbing like David's were,
our prayers may be all over the map. One minute we may
be crying, "Oh Jesus, help them!" and the next we may be
saying, "Just make that turkey pay, Lord!"

If we'll keep fellowshipping with the Lord about it,
however, we'll ultimately reach the same conclusions
that David did. He said in the end:

"As for me, I will call upon God, and the LORD
shall save me. Evening and morning and at noon
I will pray, and cry aloud, and He shall hear my
voice. He has redeemed my soul in peace from the
battle that was against me...Cast your burden on
the LORD, and He shall sustain you; He shall never
permit the righteous to be moved" (verses 16-18,22).

Did you notice how David referred to himself there?
He called himself *the righteous*! How could he see himself
as righteous after what he had done to Bathsheba and

Uriah and Tamar? Had he forgotten those transgressions? Did he think he'd done everything right?

No, David didn't base his right standing with God on what he'd done. He based it on what he believed. And he believed God had forgiven him. He believed God had removed his sins from him as far as the east from the west. He believed that God had washed him, restored him, and made it as if he'd never sinned. So when Ahithophel and Absalom tried to remind him of what he'd done wrong and exact retribution, David felt no guilt. He felt no responsibility for the bitterness they'd harbored against him.

He faced the situation as an innocent man.

If we'll put our faith in Jesus, we can do the same thing. We can put behind us the shameful sins of the past. We can get rid of the guilt that follows us around telling us we deserve to be punished. We can receive by faith a veritable flood of God's forgiveness and be washed forever clean. Avoiding the path of Absalom and Ahithophel, we can take our hurts to God and let Him heal the wounds others have dealt us. We can leave the judging to Jesus and get on with the business of living a satisfied life, trusting Him to keep the books.

CHAPTER

9

Say Goodbye to Baca

"Blessed is the man whose strength is in You, whose heart is set on pilgrimage. As they pass through the Valley of Baca, they make it a spring; the rain also covers it with pools. They go from strength to strength; each one appears before God in Zion."

Psalm 84:5-7

If you're looking for a place to build a home and settle down, here's some good, scriptural advice: Don't buy property in the Valley of Baca. Although it's a place we're all familiar with—one we invariably pass through from time to time—its long-term prospects are lousy. Nobody who homesteads in Baca ever enjoys a satisfied life.

Literally translated, the Valley of Baca means the Valley of Weeping. In Psalm 84, it's used as a metaphor, but according to biblical history, Baca was once an actual place. The valley where human sacrifices were made to a demon god named Molech, it was connected with weeping,

167

pain, terror, and trouble because of the awful, agonizing things that happened there. It was a nightmarish place so filled with despair that nothing good could ever come out of it.

Why on earth would God ever choose to mention such a place in the book of Psalms?

Because He knew that from time to time we would all find ourselves in some version of it.

God knows, even if we don't, that as believers we aren't exempt from tough times. Every single one of us has to wade through some trash in our lives. Things happen that hurt us, or pressure us, or drive us toward despair. The devil wants those things to destroy us. He tells us we'll never get over them, that we might as well give up and accept our misery as the unchangeable status quo. He tries to convince us that Baca is our final destination.

Psalm 84, however, says just the opposite. It says that the blessed man, instead of parking permanently in Valley of Weeping, can adopt a passing-through mindset. Drawing his strength from God and His Word, he can see Bacaville as temporary and say, "I'm not staying here long. I'm going through this and coming out the other side. And to make the trip worthwhile, I'll believe God to turn this barren place into a luxury resort complete with swimming pools. I'll let Him take this thing the devil meant for evil and turn it into a blessing in my life."

You know as well as I do, that kind of attitude isn't prevalent among believers today. Most Christians spend their hard times thinking, meditating, and complaining about how hard the hard times are. They aren't digging through their Bibles, keeping the Word in front of their eyes, in their ears, and in their mouths, building their faith for victory. They aren't expecting to go from strength to strength. They're expecting the bad times to weaken them. To leave them limping for the rest of their lives.

Of course, not all believers react to hard times that way. Some take an entirely different approach. They believe that if they live by faith they will be blessed (which is true) and that being blessed means bypassing Baca altogether (which is *not* true). So they go into denial when they hit the city limits. They deny that things are tough. They deny that they're sick, or broke, or emotionally hurt.

They assume that's living by faith. But it's not. Real faith doesn't refuse to acknowledge a problem exists. That's dangerous. Studies have actually shown that when people contract a disease, for instance, and go into denial about it, pretending they're not sick, they get worse, not better. Their immune system, which is designed by God to recognize and fight the disease that's attacking their body, backs off and shuts down. It responds as if there's no problem and its assistance is not needed.

"But Dennis, as faith people aren't we supposed to make positive confessions?"

Yes, we are. But that doesn't mean we deny the reality of natural facts. A scriptural declaration of faith doesn't involve calling things that *are* as though they *aren't*. No, Bible-based faith does just the opposite. It follows the example of Abraham and, like God, "calls those things which do not exist as though they did."[72]

It may sound like I'm splitting hairs here, but believe me I'm not. If illness attacks your body, there's a big difference between saying, "I'm not sick," and saying, "by the stripes of Jesus I am healed!" There's a big difference between claiming to have no emotional pain and declaring that "the Lord restores my soul." No matter what kind of problems you may be facing, it won't help you to ignore them and confess that nothing is wrong. But it will change everything if you approach those problems in the light of Scripture, believing and confessing that by the power of God what's wrong is made right.

Too many precious, Christian people fail to understand that. They do the best they can to deal with the heartbreaks life has dealt them. They love the Lord and go to church but the hurt they feel inside never seems to go away. Maybe they're grieving over a broken marriage or a loved one that died too young. Maybe some traumatic childhood experience casts a stubborn shadow over their lives. As a result, they can't make the kind of progress they desire. They get stuck in one area or another.

I know what that's like because it happened to me and it took me years to notice and acknowledge it. Maybe I'm just not a very introspective guy, but after I made Jesus Lord of my life as a teenager, I didn't give much thought to the events of my past. If somebody asked me about my childhood, I'd tell them it was nothing unusual. It was pretty much like everybody else's.

[72] Romans 4:17

In many ways that's true. My family was quite normal. My parents were average, upper middle-class Americans. They considered themselves Christians and we went to church periodically even though we didn't learn much there. We prayed at meals but never any other time. We owned Bibles but didn't read them. We had a nice car, a nice house, and the other perks of affluence. As far as I knew things were fine.

Problem was, like most kids, my knowledge didn't go very far. So when I was 13 years old, busy whining about homework and household chores, I had no clue that in my father's life, things were going wrong. So wrong that in August of that year, he committed suicide.

I remember one conversation I had about it with somebody after I was saved. When I told them that my dad killed himself, they were visibly jarred. "I thought you said you had a normal childhood!" they said.

If you've ever resented the twist and turns of your own past, if you've ever envied people who seemed to have had a normal life, this may help you. There's really no such thing as normal. Statistically, the average American household consists of 2.6 people. Yet, there's not one single household in the entire nation that includes six tenths of a person. Such a thing is impossible. Therefore the average household doesn't really exist. We're all just living at different levels of abnormality. (If you've always felt abnormal maybe that will be of some comfort to you. I know it is to me.)

From my perspective, losing my dad to suicide as a young teenager was normal. It was all I knew. Everybody deals with such experiences differently, but in my case, I just accepted it and went on with my life. I put it behind me, became an enthusiastic committed Christian, a minister, and an all round secure, happy guy.

Or so I thought.

After a number of years spent studying the Word and fellowshipping with the Lord, however, I began to notice that some areas of my life didn't reflect the satisfaction and victory the Bible promises. I saw unproductive patterns in my relationships that kept them from being as fulfilling as God meant them to be. I began to realize that I'd gotten stuck without even being aware of it. Trucking down the road of life at 13 years old, I'd blown an emotional tire in the Valley of Weeping and never stopped to fix it.

No Need to Punch Pillows

What did I do about it once I noticed? First let me tell you what I didn't do. I didn't follow the goofy advice the world offers. I didn't "let it all out" by screaming and howling and crying about how terrible I feel. I didn't punch a pillow to express my anger. I didn't lie on the floor and chant while somebody stood by playing the violin. None of those things had the power to help me. They would have left me as messed up (or more so) than I was when I started.

So what I did was this: I turned to the Word of God. I opened my Bible and asked the Holy Spirit to quicken the Scriptures to me and change what needed to be changed in my soul. And you know what? He did. He led me to

Psalm 27:10: *When my father and my mother forsake me, then the LORD will take care of me.* The New Living Testament says it this way: *Even if my father and mother abandon me, the LORD will hold me close.*

I discovered right then and there that the Holy Spirit is a magnificent and proficient Counselor! I didn't have to figure out what the problem was and tell Him about it. He already knew. I had a fear of abandonment. Amazingly enough, I'd been dragging it around unawares since the seventh grade. Keeping people at a distance because I was afraid they'd leave like my father did when I needed them. Cutting off relationships when I felt threatened or insecure.

Psychologists might see it as a complex problem. But for God it was simple to fix. All I had to do was ask Him. All I had to do was open my Bible and give Him the opportunity to speak these life-changing words into the very center of my heart. "Dennis, even if your father and mother abandon you, you don't have to be afraid because I—the Almighty God, Your Creator, your Redeemer, and your Heavenly Father—will hold you close. I'll protect you. I'll deliver you. I'll give you everything you'll ever need. And I'll personally see to it that you're never, ever alone."

I'd read Psalm 27:10 many times before but that day it came alive in me by the power of God. It penetrated the very core of my soul and shifted everything. It set me free.

That's no surprise, of course. It's what God's Word is designed to do. It's designed to take us through the Valley of Baca in triumph. To turn our mourning into dancing.

"To console those who mourn in Zion, to give them beauty for ashes, the oil of joy for mourning, the garment of praise for the spirit of heaviness; that they may be called trees of righteousness, the planting of the LORD, that He may be glorified" (Isaiah 61:3).

"If the Bible has that kind of power, then why are so many Bible-believing Christians still paralyzed by the sorrowful events of their lives?" you might ask. "Why do they dwell for years in emotional deserts instead of splashing around in divine springs?"

Because just as when you're in the desert you have to dig to find water, when you're stuck in the badlands of life you have to dig in the soil of the Scriptures to tap into the truth that sets you free. You have to root around in God's written Word until, by the power of the Holy Spirit, it starts flowing and speaking to you. Sometimes we don't do that. We just keep dragging along from Sunday to Sunday. Trying to get enough spiritual refreshment from a once-a-week sermon to get us through. Looking happy on the outside when we're miserable on the inside.

I don't mean to overwork the springs of Baca analogy, but the fact is, the Bible often compares the Word of God and the Holy Spirit to water. It tells us, for instance, that like water, the Word and the Spirit cleanse us. They refresh us. They're essential to life. Those are obvious parallels. But I've noticed another, more subtle similarity. Water always seeks out the lowest point first. The Word and the Spirit of God do the same. They seek out the valleys of weeping in our lives and begin to fill us from there.

If you want to see how dramatically the water of the Spirit can transform such valleys, think about the difference a flood can make in a natural landscape. Imagine submerging a city dump in so much water that—voila!—it becomes a lake. Suddenly instead of being a haven for flies and cockroaches, people are swimming, fishing, and skiing there. They're picnicking beside it at sunset, enjoying the beauty of a place that was once the worst kind of eyesore.

Nobody would ever guess, just by looking, that buried deep underneath that lake's shimmering, rippling, refreshing expanse is the refuse of years gone by. That's the miracle of water—both natural and spiritual. If we keep the level high enough in our lives, it makes everything beautiful.

Sounds simple enough but here's the hitch. We have to start by giving the Word of God and the Holy Spirit access to our own inner landfills. We must be willing to admit, "Lord, I have a problem. This thing that happened is hurting me. It's cheating me of the satisfaction You promised. It's wrong; it's rotten; and it's starting to stink."

In other words, we have to learn a lesson from Naaman. He was a man who understood that kind of situation. He knew what it was like to watch his life become a wasteland, not just figuratively, but literally. In a day when there was no help and no natural cure for the disease, Naaman had leprosy.

Thank heaven, he also had a little Israelite servant girl working in his household. If it hadn't been for her, Naaman would have ended up on the human garbage heap. Despite his prestigious position as commander of the Syrian army, he would have died young, alone, and in dishonor. He never would have known about Elisha, whose ministry was marked by more miracles than any other Old Testament prophet. Naaman, as a Syrian, would never have considered turning to the God of Israel for help if his compassionate young housekeeper hadn't been bold enough to say, "If only my master were with the prophet who is in Samaria! For he would heal him of his leprosy."

Initially, the suggestion must have sounded peculiar to Naaman's heathen ears. *What? Seek divine intervention…through a prophet?* he must have thought. But, desperate for help, Naaman eventually decided the idea was worth a try. So he saddled up horses and camels, and accompanied by his regal entourage, he made the trip to Elisha's house.

Being a respected nobleman, he expected an appropriately noble reception. He expected Elisha to make a fuss over him and mark the occasion with some religious pomp and ceremony. But that's not what happened. Elisha didn't even bother to stick his head out the front door and offer a greeting. Instead, he "sent a messenger out to tell him to go and wash in the Jordan River seven times and he would be healed of every trace of his leprosy!" (2 Kings 5:10 TLB).

The instructions irritated Naaman so much that he got angry and stalked away.

"'Look,' he said, 'I thought at least he would come out and talk to me! I expected him to wave his hand

over the leprosy and call upon the name of the Lord his God and heal me! Aren't the Abana River and Pharpar River of Damascus better than all the rivers of Israel put together? If it's rivers I need, I'll wash at home and get rid of my leprosy.' So he went away in a rage" (verses 11-12).

To me, Naaman's reaction sounds somewhat familiar. It reminds me of how we, as believers, sometimes react when we're told that our complicated problems can be washed away by the water of God's Word. "Are you kidding?" we say. "You think the Bible can fix this mess I've found myself in? I'm dealing with some serious issues here. They can't be resolved with something as simple as Scripture!"

When we start thinking that way, we need to remember the advice Naaman's servants gave him. As he was storming away from Elisha's house, they said:

"'If the prophet had told you to do some great thing, wouldn't you have done it? So you should certainly obey him when he says simply to go and wash and be cured!'" So Naaman went down to the Jordan River and dipped himself seven times, as the prophet had told him to. And his flesh became as healthy as a little child's, and he was healed!" (verses 13-14).

According to those verses, Naaman didn't just stick his toe in the water. He didn't take a single dip and then give up because he didn't see any immediate results. No, he submerged himself in the Jordan's waters seven times which is the number of completion. He obeyed the prophet's instructions exactly and stayed with the process until the job was done.

If we'll do that with God's Word, we'll get the same results. We'll be like Naaman and become as healthy as a child—spirit, soul, and body—if we'll simply obey the instructions God has given us:

> *"My son, give attention to my words; incline your ear to my sayings. Do not let them depart from your eyes; Keep them in the midst of your heart; for they are life to those who find them, and health to all their flesh" (Proverbs 4:20-22).*

Some Bad News and Good News about Your Soul

Notice I said that we need to be healthy not just in one area but in all three areas of our being: spirit, soul, and body. Too many Christians skip the soul part. They ignore it because they assume it was taken care of when they were born again. "God saved my soul the day I received Jesus as my Lord and Savior!" they say.

Although we often use that terminology and it sounds right, scripturally it's not quite accurate.

It's our spirit that was saved through the new birth, not our soul. When 2 Corinthians 5:17 tells us that "...if anyone is in Christ, he is a new creation; old things have passed away; behold, all things have become new..." it's referring to our spirit man, or what 1 Peter 3:4 calls the "hidden man of the heart." That part of us was totally transformed the instant we were born again, but our soul which is comprised of our mind or intellect, our will, and our emotions, wasn't really changed very much.

I'm not saying our soul wasn't affected at all by our initial step of faith. When we're first saved, our emotions might be briefly touched by what God has done for us. We might feel a fresh sense of joy and peace, for instance. But as time passes, those early emotions always fade. When they do, we find that our old thought patterns, habits, and reactions haven't changed at all. Our souls are still as messed up as they ever were.

That's the downside. The upside is this: There's something we can do about it. We can obey James 1:21 which tells us to *receive with meekness the implanted word, which is able to save your souls.* Written to believers who had already put their faith in Jesus, that verse isn't instructing people to believe the Gospel and get born again. It couldn't be. The entire passage is talking to Christians. It's informing people whose spirits have already been saved that their souls still need saving and that they can activate the process by hearing and obeying God's Word.

"For if anyone is a hearer of the word and not a doer, he is like a man observing his natural face in a mirror; for he observes himself, goes away, and immediately forgets what kind of man he was. But he who looks into the perfect law of liberty and continues in it, and is not a forgetful hearer but a doer of the work, this one will be blessed in what he does" (verses 23-25).

"Well, I read the Bible and do what it tells me to do the best I can," somebody might say, "but it doesn't seem to be making much difference. My emotional landfills still look pretty much the same."

Then ask the Holy Spirit for some extra help. Ask Him to peel back a little topsoil so that you can see what's hiding under there and identify the real cause of the problem. Maybe you need Him to bring to your attention some things that you've forgotten or overlooked so that you can apply the Word, on purpose and by faith, to those specific situations.

If that idea scares you, remember that God loves you. He's not some Supernatural Psychiatrist who gets paid by the hour to tell you what's wrong with you. He's your Father. His heart is unspeakably tender toward you. He loves you as much as He loves Jesus.[73]

Actually, that's what the New Covenant is all about. The Old Covenant was a commandment for us to love God. The New Covenant is a revelation that God loves us. The Apostle John put it this way: "This is real love. It is not that we loved God, but that he loved us and sent his Son as a sacrifice to take away our sins" (1 John 4:10 NLT). John had such a rich revelation of that fact he referred to himself as *the disciple whom Jesus loved*. That may sound to you like a brash thing to say, but the fact is, you have just as much right to say it as John did. You too are the disciple Jesus loves!

That's why you can fearlessly invite Him into those places in your heart where you've been hurt. He's not going to expose you. He's not going to criticize you and hammer you for your faults. He's not going to give somebody a

---

[73] John 17:23

word of knowledge about some embarrassing aspect of your life and leave you feeling humiliated and ashamed.

Never! God is love; and the Bible says that *love covers*.[74] It doesn't expose our imperfections, it protects and hides them. Not by pretending they don't exist but by engulfing them with love and divine power so that whatever is wrong can be made right. When God uproots the thorny issues in our lives, He does it because He doesn't want them to hurt us anymore. He wants to wash the recesses of our wounded soul with the cleansing, restoring power of His Spirit and His Word so that our Bacas can become places of blessing.

That's what He did for me with my dad's suicide. He pulled back the layer of denial I'd used to protect myself from the pain of it, and—when I gave Him the opportunity—He pointed out all the problems that denial had caused in my life. Problems I'd never paid any attention to.

Once I acknowledged them, it didn't take Him long to reveal the cause, restore that area of my soul with the power of His Word, and give me a whole new sense of freedom. Today I can say the sense of abandonment that once dogged my steps has been completely conquered. All the grief, all the feelings of loss and anger are permanently gone. They're not a part of my thinking anymore.

If any of those negative feelings try to pop back up again, I refuse to submit to them. I remind myself of the Word God quickened to me and rejoice over it. Sure, I still have memories of what happened, but they don't push my buttons anymore. They don't control me and re-ignite

---

[74] Proverbs 10:12

those dreaded emotions. Quite the opposite. They remind me of God's faithfulness and power to heal even the deepest hurts. They remind me that the water of God's Word has beautified my life so that I can stand tall and strong without any sense of guilt or shame about my past.

"But Dennis, why would you ever feel any guilt or shame about your father's suicide? You didn't cause it."

I know, but emotions aren't always logical. Especially when we're children, we often take responsibility for things that aren't our fault at all. Some kids grow up feeling guilty about their parents' divorce, for example. Even though they know better with their brain, somewhere deep in their hearts they struggle with the feeling that maybe they could have done something to help keep their parents together.

Looking back, I realize now that I was afraid my dad's choice might have meant something about me. I hid what happened from other people because I worried about how they might react if they found out. *What will they think of me?* I wondered.

We all stumble over that question at one time or another. Even though there's nothing we can do about it, we spend ridiculous amounts of energy stewing over other people's opinions of us. We base decisions and tailor our lives around what "they" might think. Of course, for the most part we don't even know who "they" are. And if we don't know who they are, we're certainly never going to figure out what they're thinking. So the whole thing is a waste of time anyway. What's more, the vast majority of people we're worried about aren't thinking about us at all. They're too concerned with themselves and their own problems to give any thought to what's going on with us.

I can almost hear somebody sobbing, "are you saying they don't care about me?"

Yes, that's what I'm saying. But if you'll let God restore your soul, their lack of concern won't depress you. You'll be so liberated that you won't care that they don't care. You'll be so busy enjoying the pools of God's blessings that other people's opinions—or lack of opinions—about you won't bother you a bit.

I know it may sound too good to be true but, I assure you, God can actually make you that free. He's an absolutely amazing therapist! So why not let Him get to work in your life? If you've been stuck in the valley of Baca, ask Him to reveal what's been holding you there.

Whatever it is, the Holy Spirit can liberate you from it. He can quicken the Word of God to you and renew your mind so that painful thing can no longer dominate your thinking. He can wash through your emotions and make them healthy and whole again. He can even take that destructive experience and turn it around for good.

He can do for you what He did for David when he was a young shepherd boy watching his flocks on the hills of Israel. Rejected when he was just a child, David hit hard times early in his life. His father, Jesse, sent him out to take care of the sheep and so thoroughly forgot about him that when the renowned prophet Samuel came to the house to anoint one of his sons to be king, Jesse didn't even call David in from the field. I don't know if David's existence totally slipped Jesse's mind on that auspicious occasion, or if he just considered his youngest boy unworthy of such an honor. But either way, it must have hurt.

No wonder David included in his psalms those life-changing words: *When my father and my mother forsake me, then the LORD will take care of me.* He wasn't just waxing spiritually poetic, he was speaking from experience. As a knobby-kneed kid, he'd found himself alone and forsaken in the Valley of Baca. He'd experienced things that, according to principles of modern psychology, should have left him angry and bitter, rebellious and withdrawn.

But as we all know, that's not how David turned out. He didn't buy property and spend the rest of his life in that emotional desert. Instead, he met God there. Surrounded by bleating sheep, he relaxed on a grassy creek bank, sunk his sun-scorched feet in a chilly stream, and sang:

"The LORD is my shepherd; I shall not want. He makes me to lie down in green pastures; He leads me beside the still waters. He restores my soul; He leads me in the paths of righteousness for His name's sake. Yea, though I walk through the valley of the shadow of death, I will fear no evil; for You are with me; Your rod and Your staff, they comfort me. You prepare a table before me in the presence of my enemies; You anoint my head with oil; my cup runs over. Surely goodness and mercy shall follow me all the days of my life; and I will dwell in the house of the LORD forever" (Psalm 23:1-6).

No question about it, David spent some time in his own personal valley of weeping. But here's what made him great: he didn't stay there. He passed through. When he left it in his rearview mirror, it looked different than it did when he arrived. No longer a place of sorrow, it was a place of joy. A place where he went from strength to strength on his way to a satisfied life.

CHAPTER 10

Keep Sowing...
and Don't Get Distracted
by the Storms

He who observes the wind will not sow, and he who
regards the clouds will not reap.

Ecclesiastes 11:4

A certain amount of predictability is a good thing. At least, God seems to think so and I'm very grateful for it. This world is challenging enough as it is. Imagine how complicated things would be if, in a burst of divine spontaneity, God had dispensed with the dependable principles of the universe. Think how many difficulties we'd face if He'd exchanged natural laws—like gravity, for instance—for a more free-wheeling system.

Personally, I appreciate the assurance that what goes up must come down. I enjoy not having to wonder if the next step will send me floating off into space. I'm a big fan of the law of gravity. It simplifies my life.

So does the law of sowing and reaping. Like gravity, it's such a foundational principle that most people take it for granted. It rarely occurs to anybody what a headache it would be for farmers if the cotton seeds they planted unexpectedly grew up to be peach trees. Or for suburban-ites, if they planted Bermuda and got a yard full of broc-coli. Or for health aficionados if the wheat grass growing on the windowsill busted out the window by producing watermelons.

No question about it, this world would be a mess if seeds could morph without warning and produce any kind of harvest they wanted. So it's a good thing they can't. It's a good thing God imposed on them a more predict-able plan and established from the very beginning that "seeds will produce the kinds of plants and fruits they came from" (Genesis 1:11 NLT). We can all be thankful that the principle of "seedtime and harvest"[75] provides us with absolute assurance that "whatever a man sows, that he will also reap" (Galatians 6:7).

Even if you're not a farmer, even if you shun yard work, the law of sowing and reaping is working for you every day of your life. Because, according to the Bible it applies not only to literal seeds and their corresponding crops but to everything else as well. The Phillips transla-tion of Galatians 6:7 makes that crystal clear. It says,

---

[75] Genesis 8:22 NKJV: "While the earth remains, seedtime and harvest, cold and heat, winter and summer, and day and night shall not cease."

"A man's harvest in life will depend entirely on what he sows."

Take finances, for example. The New Testament says that when we give financially into the work of God's Kingdom, our gifts ultimately produce a harvest of financial blessing in our own lives. In other words, when you plant money, you reap money. Second Corinthians 9 confirms it. There the apostle Paul, encouraging believers to give generously into an offering for financially-strapped fellow saints, says this:

"He who sows sparingly will also reap sparingly, and he who sows bountifully will also reap bountifully. So let each one give as he purposes in his heart, not grudgingly or of necessity; for God loves a cheerful giver. And God is able to make all grace abound toward you, that you, always having all sufficiency in all things, may have abundance for every good work...Now may He who supplies seed to the sower, and bread for food, supply and multiply the seed you have sown and increase the fruits of your righteousness, while you are enriched in everything for all liberality" (verses 6-11).

That isn't the only passage that talks about financial sowing and reaping, either. The Scriptures mention it in many other places as well. As we've already seen, the sixth chapter of Galatians speaks about it quite plainly. It reminds us to give offerings to those who minister the Word and says:

"Let him who is taught the word share in all good things with him who teaches. Do not be deceived,

God is not mocked; for whatever a man sows, that he will also reap. For he who sows to his flesh will of the flesh reap corruption, but he who sows to the Spirit will of the Spirit reap everlasting life. And let us not grow weary while doing good, for in due season we shall reap if we do not lose heart. Therefore, as we have opportunity, let us do good to all, especially to those who are of the household of faith" (verses 6-10).

Proverbs 11:25 sums up the principle this way: "The generous soul will be made rich, and he who waters will also be watered himself."

Many Christians totally overlook those scriptures and get the idea that financial increase is just a sovereign act of God. "I guess if the Lord wants me to prosper, I will" they say. "If He doesn't, I won't. My financial future is in His hands." That's not what the Bible teaches. It tells us that our financial future is in our own hands. It says that if we sow money by faith into God's kingdom, we'll reap money, multiplied, in return.

As born again believers, we need to understand that. Not so we can get rich and indulge the lusts of our flesh. Not so we can hoard up wealth in fear of the future. But so we can help advance the purposes and plans of God on the earth.

As I'm sure you've noticed, taking the Gospel to every creature is expensive! It takes cash to send missionaries all over the globe. It costs money to print Bibles and distribute them, to build and maintain church buildings, to host vacation Bible schools and minister to the poor.

Don't ever let anybody tell you God's not interested in money. He knows even better than we do that to be a financial blessing to other people, we must be blessed ourselves. He wants to prosper and increase us so that we can do the good works He has called us to do and become a visible testimony of His goodness. We're not in this for the money, we're in it for the Kingdom. We want to activate the financial law of sowing and reaping so that we can increase and be a greater blessing on this earth in Jesus' name.

If we're going to live a fully satisfied life, we're going to need plenty of money and God knows it. Yet, as much as money matters, it's not the major focus of this chapter because it's not the most important seed you're going to sow into your life. There's another kind that's far more vital.

What is it?

It's the Word of God.

The Foundation of a Successful Christian Life

Maybe you've never thought of your Bible as a sack full of abundant-life producing seed, but according to Jesus that's exactly what it is. It's not just a book of spiritual information, instructions, and encouragement. It's not just fuel for daily devotions or fodder for pastors' sermons. God's Word is spiritual seed that contains the very Life of God Himself, and it has the power to reproduce that Life (along with all of its blessings) in anyone who will plant it and keep it in the soil of their heart.

191

In Mark 4, Jesus explained in detail exactly how the process works. Describing it first in parable form, He said:

Listen! Behold, a sower went out to sow. And it happened, as he sowed, that some seed fell by the wayside; and the birds of the air came and devoured it. Some fell on stony ground, where it did not have much earth; and immediately it sprang up because it had no depth of earth. But when the sun was up it was scorched, and because it had no root it withered away. And some seed fell among thorns; and the thorns grew up and choked it, and it yielded no crop. But other seed fell on good ground and yielded a crop that sprang up, increased and produced: some thirtyfold, some sixty, and some a hundred... He who has ears to hear, let him hear! (verses 3-9)

If Jesus had concluded His teaching there, I'm sure most of us today would be like the original crowd who heard it. Leaving after the parable portion of the message, they went home scratching their heads in confusion. They had no idea what Jesus was talking about. Actually, neither did the 12 disciples. So after everybody else was gone, they asked Him what He meant.

His response was extremely revealing. "Do you not understand this parable?" He exclaimed. "How then will you understand all the parables?" (v. 13).

Obviously, Jesus regarded this particular teaching as the granddaddy of them all. It's the foundation that underlies every aspect of a successful and satisfying Christian life. To be productive in the Kingdom of God in any way, we must be able to understand and implement the process of planting the Word and getting a harvest. That's why Jesus didn't leave us in the dark about it. He shed further light on the subject by saying:

"The sower sows the word. And these are the ones by the wayside where the word is sown. When they hear, Satan comes immediately and takes away the word that was sown in their hearts. These likewise are the ones sown on stony ground who, when they hear the word, immediately receive it with gladness; and they have no root in themselves, and so endure only for a time. Afterward, when tribulation or persecution arises for the word's sake, immediately they stumble. Now these are the ones sown among thorns; they are the ones who hear the word, and the cares of this world, the deceitfulness of riches, and the desires for other things entering in choke the word, and it becomes unfruitful. But these are the ones sown on good ground, those who hear the word, accept it, and bear fruit: some thirtyfold, some sixty, and some a hundred" (verses 14-20).

Notice, Jesus described four kinds of people who hear the Word. First, He mentioned those whose hearts are so hard that the Word can't penetrate and do any good. It just sits on the surface without making a lasting impression. Although unsaved people fall into that category, surprising as it may seem, so do many Christians. Like the footpath in the parable, their heart has been packed down and hardened over because life has been tough on them. They feel like they've been walked on by everybody and everything. They go to church and hear sermons but their lives aren't changed by what they hear. They read the Bible but it bounces off without even making a dent in their problems.

If you ever find your heart in that condition, call on God and ask Him to plow your field. He can get the job done, I guarantee you. And as uncomfortable as it might be, when He's finished you'll be glad He did.

The second kind of person Jesus mentioned has what He describes as a shallow heart. Shallow-hearted Christians are often those who shout the loudest in church. When they hear the Word preached, they get excited about it. But they don't really take that Word and apply it. They don't go home and put it to work in the situations they're dealing with. They don't plant the Word firmly enough in their lives to keep the winds of adversity from blowing it away.

Shallow ground people need to learn the lesson of the palm tree. It puts down roots so deep and strong that not even a hurricane can topple it. A few years ago on a trip to Florida I got to witness that fact first hand when hurricane Fay took aim at my hotel room. She never got there because when I saw what was happening, she and I had a conversation. I told Fay that she had to change course and go somewhere else. She did and I appreciated it. In the meantime, however, I got to experience her peripheral fury up close and personal. I saw palm trees bend and sway without breaking or being swept away. I watched them survive the storm, because of their deep root system, without changing where they stood.

That's what we, as believers, should be able to do. We should be able to stand immovable on God's Word right in the middle of the storms of life. But we can't do it if we remain shallow-hearted. We have to be deeply rooted in the Word.

The third kind of person Jesus talked about suffered from an overcrowded heart. That's the person who receives the Word and implements it in his life, but before it can produce results, he gets distracted by other things. His budding faith gets choked out by worldly worries. His busy schedule leaves him no time to read his Bible. Before long, the Word fades from the forefront of his mind and takes a back seat where it exerts very little influence on his life.

The fourth person Jesus told us about was the good ground person. That's the believer who hears the Word, believes it, and refuses to let it go until it produces satisfactory results. That's the Christian who can point to their life and say, "I believed God's promise and it came to pass for me!"

Clouds, Crisis, and Barrels of Oil

I'm determined to be a good ground person, aren't you? I've made up my mind that I'm not going to let my heart get hard. I'm not going to live shallow. I'm not going get overcrowded. I'm going to be the person who enjoys the fruit of the Word he's planted.

To do that, however, I've discovered there's one major seed-sowing pitfall I must avoid. The Lord brought it to my attention a few years ago and it's found in Ecclesiastes 11:4:

"He who observes the wind will not sow, and he who regards the clouds will not reap."

That one short verse exposes one of Satan's most effective strategies. It's a strategy that can keep us from activating the powerful principle of seedtime and harvest in our lives. A strategy designed to get our eyes off the Word and onto the circumstances around us. The devil is, above all, a master distracter. He knows that if he can convince us to change our focus, he can undermine our confidence in what God has said. He can dilute our faith with fear and keep us from sowing seeds of blessing for our future.

"He who observes the wind will not sow, and he who regards the clouds will not reap."

I've seen it happen time and again to wonderful Christians. Christians who believe God is a good God. Christians who understand that He loves them and absolutely agree with everything the Bible says. They take a stand of faith on the Word and suddenly a storm arises to divert their attention. It might be an economic storm with a name like Subprime Crisis or Global Recession. It might be the latest news about the stock market or oil prices or conflicts around the world.

It's amazing how fast believers will forget about the report of the Lord and start focusing on the newscaster's report when money is involved. Shake up the economy a little and all at once, instead of giving liberally to the work of God's Kingdom, Christians are wringing their hands and tearing up their tithe check. Instead of shouting the victory over God's promises of prosperity, they're talking about the price of a barrel of oil. Before the so-called crisis

196

hit, they couldn't have cared less about oil barrels. Now those barrels are a major issue.

"Yeah, but that's understandable," somebody might say. "God doesn't expect us to stick our head in the sand. He expects us to be reasonable and use common sense."

Sure, He does. And there's nothing more reasonable—in any economy and in any circumstance—than believing and obeying God's Word. If you need proof, look at Isaac. He survived an economic crunch the likes of which we've never seen. He found himself in the midst of a national famine and a drought so severe that packing up his family and leaving his homeland appeared to be the only sane thing to do. Never mind that it was the Promised Land. To stay there meant risking the lives of Issac's entire family. Better to live in Egypt than to die in the Promised Land, he reasoned. So he made up his mind to do what all his neighbors were doing and move.

God, however, had other ideas. He appeared to Isaac and gave him a different directive. Defying all natural logic, He said:

"Do not go to Egypt…Do as I say, and stay here in this land. If you do, I will be with you and bless you. I will give all this land to you and your descendants, just as I solemnly promised Abraham, your father. I will cause your descendants to become as numerous as the stars, and I will give them all these lands. And through your descendants all the nations of the earth will be blessed" (Genesis 26:2-4 NLT).

It was a startling instruction. People all around Isaac were running for their lives from that famine-stricken country. Did God really expect Isaac to buck the trend all by himself? Did God really expect him to simply trust the Word and believe that, contrary to all natural evidence and economic indications, he could survive and even thrive in a place where there was no food or water in sight?

Yes, that's exactly what God expected of Isaac. And it's what He expects of us.

If we're going to enjoy a supernaturally satisfied life, there will be times when we'll have to do exactly the opposite of what the rest of the crowd is doing. Times when our friends go one way and we go another. Times when society is running scared and we're standing firm on the ground of God's Word. Times when we ignore the news commentators and pay attention to God, who is saying, "Do not quit believing Me. Do not stop sowing. Don't give up, change directions, or modify your course. Do what I tell you to do and you will be blessed."

When Isaac did that he was facing a life or death situation. If he stayed put and things didn't work out, he'd be burying family members before long. But, even so, he obeyed God's instructions. Then he did something else even more astonishing.

He planted seed in his Promised Land.

In the middle of a drought.

In a time of famine.

Totally ignoring the circumstances that surrounded him, the crop-scorching winds, and the rainless clouds:

"...Isaac sowed in that land, and reaped in the same year a hundredfold; and the LORD blessed him. The man began to prosper, and continued prospering until he became very prosperous; for he had possessions of flocks and possessions of herds and a great number of servants. So the Philistines envied him" (verses 12-14).

Isaac got rich right in the middle of an economic depression. He prospered when poverty was all around him. All because he kept his focus on God's Word.

Use Your Magnifying Glass

Focus is a powerful thing. I first found that out when I was just a young boy playing in my backyard in southern California. On sunny days, I'd take my magnifying glass outside on the patio and hunt for bugs. My purpose wasn't educational. My aim wasn't to learn more about them by examining them up close. I had something more destructive in mind. You see, I'd discovered that if I held the magnifying glass at just the right angle and focused sunlight on a bug, it would start to sizzle. Okay...not just sizzle, but smoke, pop, and fry. Every once in a while, a bug would even burst into flame for a second which, at 8 or 9 years old, I considered exceptionally exciting.

Granted, my perspective wasn't very spiritual. But it did give me a vivid revelation of what focus can do. Seeing the same gentle sunlight, that in its natural, diffused state made me feel so warm and cozy, focused into laser-like beams hot enough to burn not just a bug but a little boy's arm (I know because I tried it), amazed me. You might say it left an impression—in more ways than one.

When it came to faith, Isaac had that kind of laser-like focus. He magnified God's Word above everything else until it burned through every opposing circumstance and produced miraculous results. Where did Isaac learn to focus on the Word like that?

From his father, Abraham.

Talk about somebody who had to believe God's Word in the face of contrary circumstances! Abraham was the man. The first time God spoke to him, he was living in the middle of a bunch of moon-worshippers in the most heathen place you can imagine: the city of Ur which is located about 150 miles from Babylon in the area of modern day Iraq. Abraham (whose name was actually Abram back then) probably considered it a nice place to live. Under the leadership of a wicked king named Nimrod, the city had flourished. The tower of Babel had been built (well, partially built) and nobody had ever seen anything like it. Babylon and its suburbs were the happening place.

Yet the first thing God said to Abram was this. "Get out of your country, from your family and from your father's house, to a land that I will show you. I will make you a great nation; I will bless you and make your name great; and you shall be a blessing" (Genesis 12:1-2).

Ur might have seemed promising from the world's perspective but from God's perspective it was a dead end. And for Abram to fulfill the divine plan for his life, he had to separate himself from it. He had to turn his back on the influences of the godless Babylonian system because everything in it was contrary to God's way of doing things. When the Babylonians began construction on their infamous tower, for example, they said, "Let us build ourselves a city, and...make a name for ourselves."[76] They thought in terms of self-promotion, self-exaltation, and self-sufficiency. *We don't need God!* they reasoned. *We can take care of ourselves.*

When the Lord spoke to Abram, he introduced a dramatically different perspective. He said, "Obey Me and you won't have to promote yourself because I'll promote you. I'll exalt you. I'll bless you and be your sufficiency." He's saying the same thing to us today. God is calling us, just like He did Abram, to leave behind the world's way of thinking and think His thoughts instead. He's telling us to leave behind the old Babylonian way of life (which is the same as it's always been) and live by faith in Him and His Word.

I'm not suggesting God has given us the same personal directive He gave Abram. He's not telling us to literally leave our family. Although most of us do have at least one family member we'd like to escape (some people in your family might even think you're that person) God hasn't given us a biblical command to cut them out of our lives. He just wants us to turn a deaf ear to their unbelief and

---

[76] Genesis 11:4

201

live differently than they do. He wants us to follow the faith example of Abraham who:

> *"...Contrary to hope, in hope believed, so that he became the father of many nations, according to what was spoken, 'So shall your descendants be.' And not being weak in faith...he did not waver at the promise of God through unbelief, but was strengthened in faith, giving glory to God, and being fully convinced that what He had promised He was also able to perform"* (Romans 4:18-21).

I'll be honest with you. When I first read those verses, I wondered how they could say that Abraham didn't waver in his faith because in reading about his life, it seemed there were years when his faith did nothing but waver! Take the incident with Hagar, for instance. When it happened, God had already promised to give Abram and his wife, Sarah, a son. They'd believed Him for a while. But eventually, they started looking around at their circumstances and wondering how God's promise could ever be fulfilled. After all, Sarah was not only barren, she was getting old and so was Abram.

It seems to me if they'd been unwavering in their faith, they would have just acknowledged the natural facts and rejoiced in God's power to overcome them. They would have continued to sow God's Word in their hearts and expect a harvest. But that's not what they did. They started observing the wind and regarding the clouds instead. They started thinking about all the reasons why God's Word might not come to pass in their lives.

Figuring God needed some help turning Abraham into the father of even one child (much less a nation) they came up with a fleshly plan of their own. Sarah suggested to Abraham that he conceive a child with her servant, Hagar. Abraham said okay (we don't know what else he said) and, sure enough, Hagar gave birth to a son. A son who opened the door to all kinds of problems. A son who did not turn out to be the son of promise.

All this happened when Abraham was 86 years old. The next time the Lord spoke to Abram, he was 99. He'd been through 13 years of total silence. Thirteen years during which there were no scripturally recorded words from God. No further confirmations of His promise. No apparent attempts to encourage him. (That's a point worth remembering. Although God is merciful, when we decide our circumstantial storm is too much for Him to handle and try to work things out on our own in ways that contradict His Word, He's likely to get real quiet for a while.)

When God finally broke the silence, He said:

"'I am Almighty God; walk before Me and be blameless. And I will make My covenant between Me and you, and will multiply you exceedingly.' Then Abram fell on his face, and God talked with him, saying: 'As for Me, behold, My covenant is with you, and you shall be a father of many nations. No longer shall your name be called Abram, but your name shall be Abraham; for I have made you a father of many nations.'" (Genesis 17:1-3).

Although I'm not a great student of biblical numerology, I do know one very cool fact about it. The fifth letter of the Hebrew alphabet is representative of God's grace. Since His grace is what changes and empowers us, it seems significant to me that God took the fifth letter of Abram's name and exchanged it with a letter that, in Hebrew, represents God Himself.

Abraham's new name redefined him. It changed everything for him. Suddenly he began calling himself what God called him: *Father of Many Nations*. He fixed his attention completely on the divine promise he'd been given and stopped looking at the circumstances. "He did not consider his own body, already dead (since he was about a hundred years old), and the deadness of Sarah's womb."[77] He quit caring what other people thought or said. He forgot about the wind and the clouds, focused on God's Word, and the next year baby Isaac was born.

The kind of focused faith Abraham developed after his name change reminds me of something I once learned from a friend who studied karate. He was so good at it that he gave demonstrations at school assemblies, local fairs, and other kinds of gatherings. A few years ago, he was telling me about it and I couldn't resist asking, "Did you ever break stacks of bricks with your hand like people do on television and in the movies?"

"Sure, I did," he said. "Sometimes I'd stack them 10 high and split them with a single blow. I know it sounds crazy, but I did." Then he explained to me the three secrets of brick-breaking success. First, you have to know

---

[77] Romans 4:19

the right technique. Second, you have to know not just that you've been able to do it in the past but that you can do it right now. Third, you have to focus properly.

It was the third point that really caught my attention. Telling me more about it, he said, "I identify the point where I'm going to hit the top brick, then I move my focus off the top brick to a point on the floor directly below it. With my focus there on the floor, when I strike the top brick, my energy will carry me to the point of my focus."

That's how the kingdom of God works! The Holy Spirit within us takes us to the point of our focus. If our focus is on the Word, He'll take us to the point where that Word fully manifests in our life. But if our focus is on the wind and the clouds, the divine power within us will end there. If we let the contrary circumstances grab our attention and pull it off of God's promise, we won't have the spiritual energy it takes to get where we want to go.

Friend, don't let that happen to you. Don't let the devil's distractions prevent you from putting the wonderful law of seedtime and harvest to work in your life. So what if the winds blow? So what if the clouds gather? You don't have to worry about it. All you have to do is keep sowing the Word. All you have to do is keep believing God.

If you do that, your future is utterly predictable. God guarantees it. Sure as gravity, you will reap the blessings of a fully satisfied life.

Obtain the Unobtainable

So Joseph went after his brothers and found them in Dothan. Now when they saw him afar off, even before he came near them, they conspired against him to kill him. Then they said to one another, "Look, this dreamer is coming!"

Genesis 37:17-19

A few years ago when I was reading about Joseph in the Bible, the Lord spoke to my heart and said something I'll never forget. It startled me when He said it because I was caught up in the story at the time. Captivated by Joseph's God-given dreams of greatness and his brothers' murderous plot to put an end to those dreams, I was imagining the sneers on their faces as he walked innocently into their snare. Reading verse 19, I could almost hear the scorn in their voices, as they spat out their hatred for him and said, "Behold, this dreamer cometh."

That's when the Holy Spirit interrupted the story.

"Yes, Joseph was a dreamer," He said, *"and I'm getting My dreamers back!"*

I have to admit, the comment surprised me not only because of its timing but because of its content. Like most believers, I'm accustomed to the idea that God wants committed Christians. That He wants worshippers and workers who are willing to roll up their sleeves and become grace-empowered laborers in His Kingdom.

But dreamers?

Who knew that dreamers were so important to God?

I think a lot of us missed that memo. I don't know how we overlooked it. After all, the majority of our biblical heroes spent their lives pursing dreams that, if they hadn't been divinely inspired, could be rightly considered ridiculous. Think of Noah with a hammer in his hand on a mission to save mankind from a worldwide flood. Abraham, ancient, childless, and married to a barren woman, calling himself the Father of Many Nations. David expecting to be promoted from the pasture to the palace. Jabez asking to be a blessing. Gideon going up against the Midianites.

Dreamers every one of them.

Dreamers whose dreams not only changed their own lives, they changed the world.

Have you ever noticed how much we all love the stories about those heroes of faith? Even if we've heard them for years they always ignite something divine within us. Whether we admit it or not, they make us want to wave our arms and shout with a preschool enthusiasm, "I want to do something great too!"

That's because we're all divinely designed to be dreamers. We're created to cherish in our hearts the dreams God has given us. To nurture and cultivate them. To take hold of them with bulldog faith and determination—even when they look impossible—and refuse to let go.

Granted, our own personal dreams may not be as dramatic as those in the Bible. They may not involve arks or angelic visitations or supernatural name changes. Because we're born again and have the Holy Spirit living inside us, God's dealings with us are usually more subtle than that. Our dreams often start with a thought that simply keeps bubbling up within us. Or a heart-felt desire that seems unobtainable but won't go away.

We might find ourselves longing to run for political office, or spearhead an evangelistic ministry. We might envision ourselves starting a business, raising a passel of exceptional kids, recruiting volunteers to feed the poor, or solving some worldwide problem. I daresay every believer has had such dreams at some time in their life. But many of those dreams never become a reality.

Do you know why that is?

It's because we don't get what we don't go after. And most Christians don't go after—and stay after—their God-given dreams. They make the same mistake I once did. They adopt an attitude of passivity and leave everything up to God. Some years ago, I slipped into that mindset about my ministry. I began thinking that if God wanted it to flourish in a particular way, He'd just make it happen. *He's the One with all the power, I'll just let His will be done*, I thought.

That may sound good, but it's not the way God set things up. Many things He wants to happen never happen at all. He wants everybody to be saved, for instance, but they aren't.[78] Multitudes of people ignore God's will, reject salvation, and end up eternally separated from Him. It's not what God wants, but it happens anyway every day.

If it was just up to God, all of us who do get saved would grow up in Him, walk in love, live holy lives, and tell people about Jesus. But does it always happen? No, if we want to have that kind of life, we have to go after it. We must embrace God's will for us and press in to obtain it. We must follow the example of Paul who said, "I press on, that I may lay hold of that for which Christ Jesus has also laid hold of me."[79]

God won't do for us what He's required us to do for ourselves. And one thing He requires us to do is fight the good fight of faith to lay hold of the life we're called to live.[80] It's our responsibility—not His—to grab onto the promises in the Word and the Holy Ghost dreams we've been given, and hang on until they come to pass.

---

[78] 1 Timothy 2:3-4: For this is good and acceptable in the sight of God our Savior, who desires all men to be saved and to come to the knowledge of the truth.

[79] Philippians 3:12

[80] 1 Timothy 6:12: Fight the good fight of faith, lay hold on eternal life, to which you were also called and have confessed the good confession in the presence of many witnesses.

That means we have to act a lot like Duke, the Doberman Pinscher my wife and I owned in the early years of our marriage. Duke had enough locked-jaw tenacity to make a bulldog blush. When he clamped his teeth onto something, nothing could pry him loose. Always the winner at tug-of-war, he would seize his end of the rope (or his end of my sock, tie, or suit jacket) and no matter how hard I yanked he would not let go. I could throw all my weight against him. I could spin in circles until his feet left the ground and he went airborne. I could wedge my fingers in his mouth and try to wrench it open.

Through it all, Duke would drool and growl and stare at me with unrelenting eyes that telegraphed his message. *Forget it, buddy. This is my mine and you're never going to get it out of my mouth.*

Let me be clear, I'm not suggesting by this analogy that God is the one tugging against us. He's not testing our faith (as some people suggest) by trying to steal our dream. That's the devil's mission—and he's quite committed to it because our dreams are a threat to him. Divine dreams fulfilled undermine the works of darkness. So Satan fights us over them tooth and toenail. He tells us we're inferior and unworthy to walk in them. He tells us they're totally unobtainable, that there's no way they could ever become a reality.

He may even have a point. From a natural perspective, our dreams may be well beyond our reach. But, in Christ, God has given us the ability to obtain the unobtainable. We can do the seemingly impossible, if we only will. We don't have to do it in our own power, of course. God will be there for us, with us, and in us every step of the way.

He'll open doors for us. He'll lay out paths for us to take. He'll empower us with His grace. But first we must make the decision. We must dare to dream.

The Dreamer Who Decided to Go for It

That's what Joseph did. He not only dreamed, he held onto those dreams with Duke-like determination. While others allowed their circumstances to determine their identity, Joseph defined himself by his dreams.

If you've read about what happened to him, you know it wasn't easy. Holding onto dreams of greatness after he'd been sold into slavery by his brothers (who decided it would be more profitable to sell him than to kill him) couldn't have been a cake walk. Being stripped of his place as the favorite son of his wealthy father to become Potiphar's servant wasn't what you'd call a promotion. But it didn't change Joseph at all. He took the detour in stride and did his job so well that he ended up in charge of the whole place. Potiphar absolutely loved him.

But then, so did Mrs. Potiphar. For different reasons. Seeing that "Joseph was a very handsome and well-built young man…[she] began to desire him and invited him to sleep with her."[81]

Joseph declined the invitation, of course. But the woman just wouldn't give up. Day after day she pressured Joseph. "You're going to bed with me!" she said. "No I'm not," he answered. Until finally, she got mad and lied to

---

[81] Genesis 39:6-7 NLT

her husband, accusing Joseph of doing to her what she'd been doing to him.

Joseph's protests of innocence meant nothing. She was a nobleman's wife. He was a foreign slave. So He was demoted again. From estate manager to inmate. From Potiphar's mansion to a prison cell with no prospects for parole.

I don't know if Joseph put his dream on paper like some people these days do. I don't know if he mapped out a five-year plan with practical steps that would make his dream a reality. If he did, I'm sure getting locked up in an Egyptian prison wasn't part of his plan. But here's what's amazing about Joseph. He didn't let it throw him. Right there in prison, he kept believing in his dream. He kept pressing toward divine promotion and...

"Before long, the jailer put Joseph in charge of all the other prisoners and over everything that happened in the prison. The chief jailer had no more worries after that, because Joseph took care of everything. The LORD was with him, making everything run smoothly and successfully" (verses 22-23 NLT).

Along the way, Joseph made a couple of important connections: a pair of highly placed royal servants who wound up in prison on his watch and had some puzzling dreams of their own. Joseph gave them the interpretations and they went their separate ways—one to the guillotine, and the other back to his position in Pharaoh's palace. Sometime later, the surviving servant overheard Pharaoh fretting about some troublesome dreams he'd had and suggested perhaps Joseph could be of service. All the royal magicians and wise men had already tried and failed to interpret the dreams, so the suggestion seemed worth a try.

"Pharaoh sent for Joseph at once, and he was brought hastily from the dungeon. After a quick shave and change of clothes, he went in and stood in Pharaoh's presence. 'I had a dream last night,' Pharaoh told him, 'and none of these men can tell me what it means. But I have heard that you can interpret dreams, and that is why I have called for you.'" (Genesis 41:14-15 NLT).

Joseph knew right away that Pharaoh's dreams were of great national importance. They foretold seven years of abundance followed by seven years of famine. After interpreting them, Joseph offered the ruler a recommendation. He advised setting up a nationwide savings plan and said, "store up 20 percent of the grain during plenteous years, so everybody will have enough to eat during the lean years."

In the next instant, the young dreamer's persistence paid off. Because of his stubborn refusal to be defined by the actions of his betraying brothers or Potiphar's perverted wife, by slave chains or prison cells; because of his dogged determination to be defined by his dreams, he obtained the unobtainable.

"Turning to Joseph, Pharaoh said, 'Since God has revealed the meaning of the dreams to you, you are the wisest man in the land! I hereby appoint you to direct this project. You will manage my household and organize all my people. Only I will have a rank

higher than yours.' And Pharaoh said to Joseph, 'I hereby put you in charge of the entire land of Egypt.' Then Pharaoh placed his own signet ring on Joseph's finger as a symbol of his authority. He dressed him in beautiful clothing and placed the royal gold chain about his neck. Pharaoh also gave Joseph the chariot of his second-in-command, and wherever he went the command was shouted, 'Kneel down!' So Joseph was put in charge of all Egypt" (verses 39-43).

What happened to Joseph's dream-squashing brothers who so violently resented the divine vision he had for his life?

They ended up bowing down to him after all, just like Joseph dreamed they would. They didn't mind it as much as they expected, though. Because in the end it was Joseph's plan and his position of power that kept them from starving to death. It was the fulfillment of his dream that sustained not only the heathen nations in the time of famine, but the heirs of Abraham as well. Through one young man's dream, God gathered the wealth of the world into Egypt. Wealth that, some 400 years later, would be carried by the budding young nation of Israel into the Promised Land.

Can you see now why God wants His dreamers back? Can you see why He's searching for believers who will look beyond their little man-made ideas to see the supernatural plans He has for them?

God still wants to raise up leaders in the world. He wants to put His people in places of authority so He can pour His wisdom through them and bless mankind. He wants to give us ideas and solutions and inventions that bring His influence into homes, schools, communities, states, and nations. He wants to empower us to advance His mighty purposes on the earth.

Yet even so, God's big dreams for us aren't just about everybody else. He also has a vision for our personal success. He has a plan for our family and our finances and our own individual future that will thrill us and make us examples of His great love.

But for those great plans to become a reality, we have to do the same things God's dreamers did in former generations. We have to look in the Word and fellowship with the Holy Spirit until we can see what God sees for our lives. And then we have to go for it.

The Master of Breakthroughs

To be clear, I'm not suggesting we should push with the arm of the flesh to fulfill our own dreams. I'm not saying we should bust through the opposition we encounter with brainpower and brute force. That's the world's way, not ours. As believers, we pursue our dreams differently. We get our breakthroughs supernaturally.

We get them by faith and by the anointing. Like David did.

I know we've already talked about him a lot. But—with the possible exception of Joseph—he can teach us more about the scriptural process of overcoming the obstacles to our divine destiny than any other Old Testament hero.

In fact, the very term "breakthrough" can be found in the Bible only in connection with him. He's the one who came up with it.

The occasion?

One of his many confrontations with the Philistines. Right after David became king, they (predictably) attacked him and tried to put a stop to his reign.

It must have been an infuriating moment for David. After all, he'd been dreaming of kingship ever since Samuel anointed him as a youngster. He'd been holding onto that vision for decades and when God had brought it to pass, instead of celebrating, he immediately had to deal with an onslaught of fierce and furious foes. If God didn't intervene, his reign could have been over before it began.

> *"So David inquired of the LORD, saying, 'Shall I go up against the Philistines? Will You deliver them into my hand?' And the LORD said to David, 'Go up, for I will doubtless deliver the Philistines into your hand.' So David went to Baal Perazim, and David defeated them there; and he said, 'The LORD has broken through my enemies before me, like a breakthrough of water.' Therefore he called the name of that place Baal Perazim" (2 Samuel 5:19-20).*

The phrase *Baal Perazim* can be literally translated the *Master of Breakthroughs*. What a wonderful name for our God! He is, indeed, a God of breakthroughs. It's a good thing, too, because as long as the devil is running loose on planet earth, we'll need them. As long as Satan has a shot at putting a stop to our divine dreams, he'll be waging a battle of containment against us that's every bit as real as the battle the Philistines waged against David.

Of course, if you're saved, the devil has already lost that battle on a number of fronts. He failed to keep you from getting born again for instance. Don't you think he desperately wanted to prevent that? Don't you think that if he was such a hotshot on the spiritual battlefield, he would have made sure you'd never heard the Gospel and become a Christian?

Certainly he would! But he wasn't able to do it. And if he couldn't contain you back then (when you were lost and powerless), he definitely can't contain you now that you have Jesus living inside you.

He will try, however. He'll oppose you at every turn to thwart any further advancement. No matter how far you've already come, he'll say you've made all the progress you can make. That you'll never be able to overcome the obstacles you see ahead of you. That you've won some minor skirmishes in the past, but the major battles you're facing now will leave you defeated. Lying through his teeth, he'll tell you that you're permanently and hopelessly stuck.

Sadly, many Christians buy such lies and remain spiritual babies for the rest of their lives. Even though they've given their heart to Jesus and they desire to live for Him, they stay stuck in the same habits, addictions, fears, and sins that dominated their lives before they were saved. Because they don't know the power that belongs to them as believers, the devil is able to contain them. Because they haven't heard enough scriptural truth to set them free, they don't experience the victory that belongs to them in Christ.

I'll be eternally grateful that didn't happen to me. I'd hate to spend the rest of my life living like I did when I first got born again. I was a total mess back then. A long-haired kid straight off the beaches of southern California, I had a habit of smoking just about anything that burned. Once I got saved, I wanted to get rid of that habit. It doesn't take a spiritual rocket scientist to figure out that kind of lifestyle doesn't glorify God. Nobody had to tell me not to bring hash, marijuana, pills, and the rest of that trash to church with me. I knew it was wrecking my life and I was eager to get free.

Thank God, I got hold of enough truth to believe it was possible and within days, I'd totally lost interest in drugs. They weren't even a temptation to me. I'd seen in the Word that something better was available to me. So I began to pursue it. I began to chase after what God said belonged to me, determined to obtain it.

That was in 1971...and I've never stopped. I'm still pursuing God's promises because the more I obtain, the more I see He has planned for me. There's always more ground to take, more victories to be won.

If I ever thought the devil would get tired of opposing me and give me a break, I know better by now. He's still there. Fighting to contain me. Granted, he doesn't use the same strategies he used 40 years ago. Back then, he might have tried to draw me off course by offering me a joint. Today, that wouldn't be a temptation, it would be a joke. So he uses other tactics to prevent me from pressing forward. He ups the ante. Sends in more troops. Until sometimes it seems to me I'm facing a wall of resistance that looks almost impenetrable.

Which brings us back to David and the Philistines. That's what they did to him. They penned him in until there was only one way he could make any further progress. He had to have a supernatural breakthrough.

Of course, for David that was no problem. Because of his long-standing relationship with the Master of Breakthroughs, he had a history of them. A history the Philistines knew all too well. That's why they were so doggedly determined to stop him. Every single Philistine soldier that gathered against Israel's newly appointed king at Baal Perazim remembered what he'd done to them years before. They still felt the humiliating sting of what had happened when David, as just a teenager, had faced the giant of a man who'd been their greatest asset, the embodiment of the strength of their entire nation.

In the minds of the Philistines, David's breakthroughs had begun long before he became king. They'd begun on the day he faced Goliath.

But the Philistines were wrong.

As believers who want to follow David's victorious example, we need to understand that. We need to know he didn't just jump up one day because the opportunity presented itself and start slaying giants. He spent years in preparation. He developed the giant-killing, crowd-thrilling anointing that eventually made him famous, in the pasture when nobody was watching. He practiced his first exploits of faith in fields where his only admirers were four-legged wool-wearers, and the only word of praise he heard was, "Baaaa."

David was just as anointed when he was a shepherd as he was when he was crowned king. But he taught us by example that it's not enough just to be anointed. We must also learn how to live and operate in the power of that anointing. We must use the seemingly inconsequential seasons of life to grow in spiritual strength and in our knowledge of God so that when the important moments come and we face the crucial battles, we're ready.

That's what David did. He didn't spend his shepherding days just daydreaming about being king. He spent them learning how to reign. When he was out on the hillside by himself and a lion snatched one of his father's lambs, he went after it and delivered the lamb from its mouth. "And when it arose against me," he said, "I caught it by its beard, and struck and killed it."[82]

Can you picture that? A lion's beard is right under his chin! That means David stood eye-to-with that lion, less than an arm's distance away, with one hand just a few inches away from its fang-filled mouth while with his other hand he delivered a punch that would wilt Mike Tyson. Just one blow with this kid's bare fist—POW!—and the lion was dead.

That didn't happen because David was exceptionally strong or skilled. The power he used to kill that lion came

---

[82] 1 Samuel 17:35

from the anointing that was on him. It came from his confidence in his covenant with God.

Certainly the lamb was the grateful beneficiary of David's covenant confidence, but that wasn't the reason David clobbered that lion. Sorry if that messes up the story for you. I realize it makes a great pastoral message when it's told that way. It sounds very sweet and spiritual to talk about how David cared so much about one precious lamb that he risked his life for it. But that doesn't make sense to me. Yes, I'm an animal-lover and I had great affection for the puppet Lamb Chop I watched on TV as a kid. But as far as I'm concerned, if a lion wraps its lips around Lamb Chop, he can just go ahead and eat it. I'm not putting my life on the line for a piece of mutton.

Neither would David. He was brave, but he wasn't stupid. He didn't go after that lion just to deliver one lone lamb. He went after it because he was anointed to have dominion. He was anointed to be king, and his current kingdom was a flock of sheep. When the lion grabbed that lamb he challenged David's reign and David responded with righteous indignation. Refusing to let a lion steal from him, he took his first step toward obtaining the unobtainable: he punched out the king of the beasts with his bare hand.

Sometime later, a bear with an appetite for shepherd's pie wandered into the same pasture. Guess he hadn't heard about the lion. David, still pressing into the power of the anointing, turned him into a rug. I can almost hear the lambs laughing.

"Okay, Kid. Show Us What You've Got."

After those victories, David was ready for a greater challenge. He encountered it the day his father sent him out of the pasture and onto the battlefield to deliver some groceries to his military brothers. He didn't expect to become a national hero that day. He was just running an errand. Chatting with his siblings and passing out food.

Then Goliath showed up and stole the show.

A nine-foot-tall monster of a man with a head the size of a watermelon, he strode to the middle of the war zone and taunted the entire Israelite army. Throwing down the gauntlet and saying the same words he'd repeated for days, he jeered:

> *"'Why have you come out to line up for battle? Am I not a Philistine, and you the servants of Saul? Choose a man for yourselves, and let him come down to me. If he is able to fight with me and kill me, then we will be your servants. But if I prevail against him and kill him, then you shall be our servants and serve us.' And the Philistine said, 'I defy the armies of Israel this day; give me a man, that we may fight together.'"[83]*

David watched the scene unfold, wide-eyed and astonished. This couldn't be happening! Looking around at his brothers and the other Israelite soldiers who were armed, trained, and much older than he was, he waited for their response. Surely one of them would march out there and mow this bigmouth down. But nobody picked up their

---

[83] 1 Samuel 17:8-10

weapons. There was no marching. No mowing. Instead, "all the men of Israel, when they saw the man, fled from him and were dreadfully afraid."[84]

David couldn't believe his eyes. *This man has no God-given anointing,* he thought. *He has no covenant with the Almighty. So what if he's as strong as a grisly? So what if he looks big and bad? What's big and bad just falls and makes a louder noise! Why is this travesty being tolerated?*

Too steamed to restrain himself, David erupted with indignation, "Who is this uncircumcised Philistine, that he should defy the armies of the living God?"[85]

I love that statement. I think it's one of the most thrilling, faith-packed sentences in the Bible. David's eldest brother Eliab, however, had a different opinion. He thought it sounded like the boasting of a presumptuous little punk. Figuring David was still full of himself because Samuel picked him over the rest of the family to be the future king, Eliab decided to put him in his place. "What are you doing around here anyway?" he demanded. "What about those few sheep you're supposed to be taking care of? I know about your pride and dishonesty. You just want to see the battle!"[86]

David was a nicer guy than I am. I would have said, "What battle? There's no battle going on here. None of you milquetoast, wet-noodle wimps has lifted so much as a finger to fight!"

---

[84] Verse 24
[85] Verse 26
[86] Verse 28 NLT

But David didn't say that. He just began to talk about the anointing that was on him. He talked about his covenant with God and his former victories. He told everybody who would listen about the lion and the bear until eventually even Israel's King Saul heard about it.

Relieved to find somebody with enough guts to fight, Saul turned the young shepherd loose. "Show us what you've got, kid," he said. "The giant is yours for the taking. Go get him!"

In Hollywood's version of the story, David trembled with fear over what he was facing. He fretted and fidgeted and hoped he'd survive. But that's not the picture painted in the Bible. It says David picked up his five rocks, put them in a pouch, and headed straight for Goliath—shouting the whole time. Unfazed by his opponent's bellowing threats, he squared off against him and made an announcement that should have sent a shiver down every Philistine spine.

"You come to me with a sword, with a spear, and with a javelin. But I come to you in the name of the LORD of hosts, the God of the armies of Israel, whom you have defied. This day the LORD will deliver you into my hand, and I will strike you and take your head from you. And this day I will give the carcasses of the camp of the Philistines to the birds of the air and the wild beasts of the earth, that all the earth may know that there is a God in Israel. Then all this assembly shall know that the LORD does not save with sword and spear; for the battle is the Lord's, and He will give you into our hands" (verses 45-47).

That's the last thing Goliath ever heard. A split second later a stone from David's sling sailed into his forehead and felled him like a lumber-jacked tree. With one rock, Goliath was finished.

David, however, was just getting started. While the Philistine army watched in horror, he grabbed Goliath's sword, pulled it out of its sheath, and cut off his melon-sized head. Then, lifting the gruesome thing in the air, swinging blood and eyeballs and hair all over the place, he carried it like a trophy all the way back to Jerusalem.

Any way you cut it (pardon the pun), David made an open display of the greatness of his God that day. He not only got the victory in that seemingly impossible situation, he took another crucial step toward his destiny. He obtained the unobtainable.

The process may not have been pretty. But when it was done, it was such a testimony of the glory and power of God it stirred up the entire Israelite army. With a great shout of triumph, they "rushed after the Philistines, chasing them as far as Gath and the gates of Ekron... Then the Israelite army returned and plundered the deserted Philistine camp."[87]

Watching David reminded his fellow Israelites of what was available to them through the anointing and covenant they had with the Almighty. Any one of them could have killed Goliath. They had the same divine covenant that David did. Any of the soldiers in God's army could have been the hero that day but they weren't ready.

[87] Verses 52,53 NLT

They didn't know what God would do through them. The only one who did was a baby-faced shepherd.

Sadly, the story today is often the same. When Goliath shows up, most Christians aren't ready. Unfamiliar with their covenant, all they know to do is run and hide. But there are always a few Davids who rise up in faith and conquer. They seem to breeze through major problems so smoothly that others think they're Super Christians. But they're not. They're just regular believers who have meditated on God's Word and practiced operating in His anointing in their everyday lives. They're normal people who found out what's available to them in Christ before the crisis hit.

It's a good thing to know where you stand before you face the enemy. Victory comes more easily when you learn in advance how to access God's strength. Smart believers take advantage of the lessons that can be learned in times of preparation with the lions and the bears.

Don't get me wrong. If you're not ready when the crisis comes, God will still find a way to deliver you if you'll look to Him. He's always on your side. He's always there for you whether you've developed your spiritual skills or not. It's just a lot better, a lot easier, when you find out sooner rather than later about the God you serve. The victories are much more glorious when you know the divine power that's backing you before you face the battle.

The fight is a lot more fun when you can shout with confidence like David did, "This isn't going to end in destruction! This isn't going to end in defeat! It's going to end with the devil running for cover, while I stand in triumph with a trophy in my hand!"

Back to Baal Perazim

Goliath had spent years in his grave by the time the Philistines gathered at Baal Perazim to end David's kingship and take their revenge. This time they didn't send just one representative. They swarmed against him by the thousands.

Although I've never faced that exact situation, I have an idea what David felt like that day. There was a day a few years ago when the entire North American continent got a respite from spiritual warfare because every devil within a thousand miles was at my house. They were too busy harassing me to bother anybody else. At least, that's how it felt. I'm sure you've had days like that too. Days when things looked so dark and the situation you faced loomed so menacing that your mind staggered. Victory seemed beyond the reach of reason. And your brain drew a blank with no idea what to do.

Chances are, you know this already. But in case you don't, I'll tell you: human beings do foolish things at times like that. We mentally amp out and get absolutely goofy. Why? Because we're not designed by God to handle those kinds of situations with our soul. We're designed to handle them with our spirit, with the divine wisdom that flows directly from God into our inner man.

That's why we need to take a cue from David. When the enemy rose up against him, he didn't just put on his thinking cap and try to figure out what to do. He didn't look out at that seething sea of Philistine soldiers, grit his teeth, and try to tough it out. He did something much wiser, he "went down to the stronghold...[and] inquired of the LORD."[88]

A former Jebusite fortress that had been conquered by Israel, the stronghold was a place of safety for David. A place where he could go with confidence and hear God's voice. David knew that's what he needed. Even though he'd experienced some victories in the past, even though he'd been a warrior for a while now and he knew what he was capable of doing, that wasn't enough. He didn't need to know what he could do at that moment; he needed to know what God wanted him to do.

Sure enough, David received exact instructions. God told him to go after his enemies, to take on a battle that appeared to be impossible to win, and win it anyway by putting his faith in the power and promise of God.

"Go up," He said, "for I will doubtless deliver the Philistines into your hand."

In the realm of the spirit, the victory was already a done deal. God had given His Word. The battle was already won. David's part was to believe what God had said, reach into the spiritual realm by faith, and bring that victory into the earth. So that's what he did.

If we want to obtain the unobtainable, we have to do the same thing, and God has fully equipped us for the job. Through Jesus, He's given us free access to the realm of the spirit. He's given us the ability to hear from the

---

[88] 2 Samuel 5:17,19

Holy Spirit and operate in His divine power. Through His Word, He's revealed to us all the spirit-realm victories that, in Christ, have already been won. And through faith, He enables us to take hold of those victories so they can become a tangible reality in our earthly lives.

So what are we waiting for?

Let's start dreaming our God-given dreams. Let's look the impossible squarely in the eye and follow in the footsteps of Joseph and David. Let's...

- Grab hold of God's promises with bulldog faith and refuse to let go.

- Cultivate His anointing in our lives and our confidence in His covenant.

- Seek His wisdom.

- Go up against the enemy and obtain the unobtainable.

You don't have to defer your divine destiny any longer. I can tell you from the Scriptures, your time has come. As Mark 1:15 says, "This is a moment of fulfillment. The manifestation of God's purpose is breaking through. Change your attitude about yourself and about God and believe the Good News!"[89] The Master of Breakthroughs is getting His dreamers back...and one of those dreamers is you.

---

[89] Paraphrase from *The Heart of Paul* by Ben Campbell Johnson; A Great Love, Inc., Taccoa, GA.

CHAPTER

Fall into Greatness

Do not gloat over me, my enemies! For though I fall, I will rise again. Though I sit in darkness, the LORD himself will be my light.

Micah 7:8 NLT

Everything I know about trapeze artists, I learned from a peculiar little article I stumbled across a few years ago. An interview with a performer about how he learned his craft, it wasn't written from a spiritual perspective. Yet when I read it, I discovered a fascinating fact that every Christian who aspires to fulfill God's lofty plans for their lives needs to know:

The key to flying high is learning how to fall—*with confidence.*

It sounds a bit backward, I know. But, according to the article, that's the first lesson all successful trapeze artists must learn.

Before they can sail from trapeze to trapeze at heart-stopping heights, they must first conquer their fear of falling. They must swing skyward and let go...swing skyward and let go...until they can rest assured that every time they drop, the net will be there to catch them. That they can trust it without question. That they can fly free without fear because no matter what happens, they will be all right.

The better a trapeze artist learns that lesson, the less often he will fall.

Why is that important to us, as believers?

Because we, too, have a net stretched beneath us. It's a safety net of grace set in place by our loving God. It's a net designed to catch us when, reaching upward toward our divine dreams, we lose our grip and drop like a rock.

Although we don't like to dwell on it, we all know what that's like. We've all taken a tumble or two from the heights of victory to the depths of defeat, not because God failed us or because His Word didn't work, but because we somehow messed things up. Maybe there was something we didn't know. Maybe we didn't have the spiritual strength and maturity we needed at the time. Maybe we just plain made a mistake.

Whatever the reason, every one of us has been there, and many believers so dread going there again that they've chosen to play it safe. To live permanently in the lowlands. Where there are no dreams. Where there is no satisfaction. Where there is no possibility of plummeting from the heights.

The solution would make sense if it was actually the skyward swing of faith that threatened our safety. We would be wise to lower our expectations—to reach for earthly possibilities instead of divine promises—if going higher is what caused us to crash. But it's not. What brings us down is the same thing that brings down the inexperienced trapeze artist.

The fear of falling.

It breaks our focus. It interrupts our concentration. It eclipses the Word, causes our faith to fail, and there's only one way to whip it. We must develop our confidence in God's grace net. We must discover its amazing power to protect us when we plummet and buoy us back up again to ever greater heights. We must realize that God has made it possible for us to literally fall into greatness.

Although falling into greatness sounds like an oxymoron, people in the Bible did it all the time. Take the apostle Peter, for instance. He was a true spiritual trapeze artist. He could fall from the pinnacle to the pit in seconds flat. He could be in God's glory on the Mount of Transfiguration one minute, and be saying something utterly ridiculous the next, simply because "he didn't know what else to say."[90] Yet Jesus chose him anyway to do great things in the kingdom of God.

That's why Peter is one of my favorite disciples. He's like the rest of us. He didn't always get things right the first time around. He often aimed for the clouds and ended up in the dirt. His life provides us with multiple

---

[90] Mark 9:6 TLB

illustrations of what can happen when a believer sets his sights on the extraordinary and misses it.

Think about what happened on the Sea of Galilee, for example, when Jesus called Peter to walk with Him on the water. That walk has inspired Christians for 2,000 years! Granted, Peter didn't finish it perfectly, but at least he started it. That's something none of the other disciples were willing to do. They were too panic-stricken to even consider it. When they saw Jesus strolling across the waves toward their boat, all they could think about was ghosts! All they could do was cry out for fear.

"But immediately Jesus spoke to them, saying, 'Be of good cheer! It is I; do not be afraid.' And Peter answered Him and said, 'Lord, if it is You, command me to come to You on the water.' So He said, 'Come.' And when Peter had come down out of the boat, he walked on the water to go to Jesus" (Matthew 14:27-29).

Peter had some character flaws, but passivity wasn't among them. He was the only one in the boat that night who was ready to jump into the middle of a stormy sea. He was the only one who looked at what Jesus was doing and said, "Hey, I want to do that too!"

Jesus didn't rebuke him for it, either. He encouraged him. He said, "Come on out here! Let's see what your faith can do."

I don't claim to know for sure what Peter felt like when he got out on the waves, but I do have a hunch because I've been there myself. Not walking, of course, but on a surf board. Back in my beach boy days, I used to paddle out into the ocean hoping to catch a (relatively) sizable wave, and when I saw one coming, I'd get excited. I'd go after it with all my might thinking, *Yeah! I want to do this!* But when I hit the crest and looked down, my excitement occasionally turned to momentary panic and I'd think, *Why am I doing this?*

That's what happened to Peter. He took his first few steps on the sea while the other disciples watched in wonder. "But when he saw that the wind was boisterous, he was afraid; and beginning to sink he cried out, saying, 'Lord, save me!'"[91]

I don't know how long it takes other people to sink, but in my experience, sinking takes almost no time at all. The beginning and the end of my sinking have always been very close together. I assume that was the case for Peter too because the instant he yelped for help, "Immediately Jesus stretched out His hand and caught him, and said to him, 'O you of little faith, why did you doubt?'"[92]

The next thing Peter knew, he was back in the boat. That's a good place to be, especially when sinking is the last thing you remember. Personally, as an aspiring water-walker (metaphorically, I mean) I take comfort in the knowledge that Jesus has no trouble getting us back into the boat. He's an expert at it. He's in the business of lifting us up when we need it. He's not in the business of putting us down. He doesn't shake His head and say, "Too bad your faith failed you. You've really blown it now.

[91] Verse 30
[92] Verse 31

I hope you're a strong swimmer, otherwise you're going to drown."

No, that's not what Jesus says. That's what man-made religion says. It criticizes people while they sink. It condemns folks for getting so excited about walking by faith that they get in over their head. Religion is hard on people and requires them to pay for their mistakes. Jesus does just the opposite. He reaches out and rescues them so they can live and learn and walk on water another day.

Like Peter did.

More Lessons from a Frequent Faller

Well, to be technically accurate, Peter didn't literally walk on water again. But he did keep jumping out of the proverbial boat. He did step out by faith with boldness while others hung back. We see proof of it in Matthew 16. There, Jesus asked the disciples, "Who do you say that I am?" and Peter was the only one daring enough to answer.

"You are the Christ, the Son of the living God," he boomed.

The others waited with lumps in their throats to see if the answer was right. But Peter wasn't worried. Having survived his dip in the sea, he'd developed new confidence in the grace net. He was secure enough to blurt out what he believed even if it meant risking another fall. This time, however, he stayed upright. His faith stood firm and his revelation was correct. Instead of catching him, Jesus congratulated him and said:

"Blessed are you, Simon Bar-Jonah, for flesh and blood has not revealed this to you, but My Father who is in heaven. And I also say to you that you are Peter, and on this rock I will build My church, and the gates of Hades shall not prevail against it. And I will give you the keys of the kingdom of heaven, and whatever you bind on earth will be bound in heaven, and whatever you loose on earth will be loosed in heaven" (Matthew 16:17-19).

At that moment, Peter was flying high. Sailing the spiritual stratosphere. Basking in the glow of being blessed by the Master for uttering a truth so vital that it would become the eternal bedrock of God's kingdom on earth.

Knowing Peter, he probably figured right then that his grace net days were over. He wouldn't need it anymore. He'd outgrown failure and would never fall again.

If that's what he thought, he was quickly proven wrong. Just three verses later we find him making one of the most bone-headed remarks recorded in Scripture. We find him actually scolding Jesus for His negative point of view! What prompted him to do such a thing? Jesus' statements about how the plan of redemption was about to unfold. Peter refused to believe that the sufferings Jesus described and His impending death on the cross were really necessary. So, after being the mouthpiece of divine wisdom the moment before, he suddenly became the instrument of the devil. He actually took Jesus aside, rebuked him (can you imagine such a thing?) and said, "Far be it from You, Lord; this shall not happen to You!"

This time, instead of getting rewarded for his revelation, Jesus turned to him and said, "Get away from me, Satan! You are a dangerous trap to me. You are seeing things merely from a human point of view, and not from God's."[93]

Here again, Peter had slipped into some serious sinkage. Without realizing it, he'd put a stumbling block in front of Jesus by suggesting he should avoid the crucifixion. Jesus was just as human as we are. His flesh would have preferred to opt out of suffering. What Peter said represented a real temptation to Him. So He responded with vigor. First, he addressed Satan, who'd duped Peter into being his pawn. Then He told Peter that he'd stepped out of the realm of revelation and gone down the path of human logic.

Clearly, there's nothing wrong with logic in itself. Common sense is a good thing and not nearly as common as it should be. But Peter needed to learn, as we all do, when we're endeavoring to follow the plan of God, the logical route isn't always the right one. There are times when our own human reasoning will take us down the wrong path.

Apparently, that was a hard concept for Peter to grasp, because even after Jesus corrected him, he kept on galloping in that direction. He was still going that way some days later in the Garden of Gethsemane when the Roman soldiers and Jewish leaders came to arrest Jesus. Still clinging to his logical plan to save the Savior from

---

[93] Verse 23 NLT

His suffering, Peter tried to stop them. He drew his sword and cut off a man's ear!

Most of us know it when we've fallen. We recognize right away when we're in need of the net. Not Peter. (Isn't it comforting to know that someone who turned out as well as he did was initially such a slow learner?) He viewed his courage as commendable. He saw it as proof that the boast he'd made at the Passover supper was true. When Jesus had warned him then that the devil was about to turn him into a coward, Peter had replied, "Lord, I am ready to go with You, both to prison and to death." Now, his swashbuckling in Gethsemane convinced him he was right. He was, indeed, the ultimate defender of His Lord.

The illusion didn't last long, however. Within hours, instead of defending Jesus, Peter found himself denying Him.

How did he stumble into such a dizzying fall? The same way we do. He compromised a little bit at a time. He started by taking a step back from the Master. As Luke 22:54 explains, when the authorities arrested Jesus and brought Him to the high priest's house, "Peter followed at a distance."

You know as well as I do, he's not the only disciple who's made that mistake. Many of us have followed the Lord at a distance from time to time. When the going got rough and it looked like the price of doing things His way might cost us more than we want to pay, we've slacked off a little. We've gotten casual about our Christianity. We cut back on our time in the Word and in prayer. And because it's impossible to stay close to Jesus by accident, we, too, have found ourselves following at a distance.

In the beginning that kind of compromise seems like no big deal. *So what if our passion for the Lord cools off a little?* we think. *Where's the harm in that?*

Peter can tell you. He found out that when you get cold, you start looking for someplace to warm up. If you're not close to the Lord, you're likely to choose the wrong place. That's what he did the night of Jesus' arrest. He didn't know he was headed toward catastrophe. He just needed a little heat, a little light, and maybe a little conversation. So when he came upon a gaggle of unbelievers who had kindled a fire in Caiaphas's courtyard, "Peter sat among them."[94] He warmed by the wrong fire.

Don't misunderstand. I'm not saying he should have avoided those unbelievers altogether. I'm not suggesting that as Christians we should be isolationists. God hasn't called us to be hermits and live in a cave so that we can be holy. On the contrary, God loves sinners and wants us to reach out to them, even rub elbows with them, whenever we can so that we can show them His love. But that wasn't Peter's mindset. He wasn't looking for an opportunity to evangelize, he was looking for an escape from the pressures of discipleship.

Sometimes believers do the same thing today. I've even heard them justify it by criticizing other Christians. "I can't relax around church people," they say. "I'd rather be with my unsaved friends. They make me feel more comfortable."

---

[94] Verse 55

"Of course, they do!" I want to answer. "When you're with unbelievers you don't feel you have to measure up to anything. They have no spiritual standard in their lives. Because they're not pursuing the things of God at all, they make your lukewarm relationship with Him look perfectly all right!"

That was Peter's problem when he warmed by the wrong fire. Instead of influencing the unbelievers around him, he let them influence him. He became hotter on the outside but cooler on the inside until, without warning, he slipped into a situation he would deeply regret.

It happened when one of his unbelieving companions, a servant girl, noticed him in the firelight and recognized him. "This man was one of Jesus' followers!" she said.

"Peter denied it. 'Woman,' he said, 'I don't even know the man!' After a while someone else looked at him and said, 'You must be one of them!' 'No, man, I'm not!' Peter replied. About an hour later someone else insisted, 'This must be one of Jesus' disciples because he is a Galilean, too.' But Peter said, 'Man, I don't know what you are talking about.' And as soon as he said these words, the rooster crowed. At that moment the Lord turned and looked at Peter. Then Peter remembered that the Lord had said, 'Before the rooster crows tomorrow morning, you will deny me three times'" (Luke 22:57-61 NLT).

This time Peter wasn't sinking, he was sunk. In one horrible moment, he'd ruined everything he'd worked for in the previous three and a half years. He'd betrayed His beloved Lord in His darkest hour. He'd shown himself to be totally unworthy of His trust.

Drowning in condemnation, crushed by the realization that his own fleshly weakness had destroyed all hope for his future, Peter did the only thing he could think of to do. He left the courtyard, crying bitterly.[95]

Two Words that Changed Everything

If we didn't know the end of the story, even those of us who know God's goodness and Jesus' saving grace might wonder how anyone could ever recover from such a devastating fall. After all, many Christians these days don't. They blunder into failure or make a bad decision and spend the rest of their lives on the spiritual ash heap. Convinced their flaws have condemned them to a lowly future, they give up their great, God-given dreams and live the rest of their lives with a broken heart.

That's what would have happened to Peter if Jesus hadn't been there to catch him with the grace net. His life would have faded from the Scriptures. We never would have heard about him again if Jesus hadn't turned the whole tragedy around with two life-changing words.

Two words. That's all it took to catapult Peter from rock bottom to sky high. He didn't have to spend a decade or two on probation paying penance for what he'd done and working himself back into God's good graces. All he had to do was listen and respond to the simple message

---

[95] Luke 22:62

Jesus delivered through the angel to two women who showed up on Sunday morning at the empty tomb.

"Do not be alarmed. You seek Jesus of Nazareth, who was crucified. He is risen! He is not here. See the place where they laid Him. But go, tell His disciples — and Peter — that He is going before you into Galilee; there you will see Him, as He said to you" (Mark 16:6-7).

That message was a thriller for all of Jesus' followers. But for the brawny fisherman who thought he'd disqualified himself from discipleship completely, it carried extra meaning. It rocked his world to hear that Jesus had included him specifically, by name.

Tell the disciples...and Peter.

And Peter!

Can you imagine how wonderful those words must have sounded? How Peter's spirit must have leapt? Standing there with his friends who'd been more faithful to the Lord than he. Feeling so ashamed and unworthy to be counted among them; remembering the moment he'd locked eyes with the Master after he'd cursed and denied Him; Peter's first thought, when he heard Jesus was alive, must surely have been, *Will He ever want me back?*

With two simple words, Jesus had answered the question. He'd lifted Peter from the depths of despair, just as He'd lifted him out of the storm-swept sea. The meaning behind His message was unmistakable. As far as Jesus was concerned, nothing had changed between Him and his beloved frequent faller. Peter's place with Him was still the same. All Peter had to do to step back into it was believe and act upon that truth. All he had to do was show up to meet the Master and it would be as if nothing had ever happened. Leaving his cowardly plunge behind, he could go on to stand on the streets of Jerusalem, anointed by Pentecostal fire, and preach messages that would sweep thousands into God's kingdom.

Now that's what I call falling into greatness! And it's the kind of thing that can happen not just to Peter but to us! No matter how miserably we've messed up, God can still do great things in us, and for us, and through us. He can turn our setbacks into promotions. He can turn our tumbles into triumphs. But only if we take the attitude of the prophet Micah and say:

> *"Do not rejoice over me, my enemy; when I fall, I will arise; when I sit in darkness, the LORD will be a light to me" (Micah 7:8).*

That's what Peter chose to do. He didn't hang around in the pit having a pity party. He didn't whine and say, like the lady on the infamous commercial, "I've fallen and I can't get up!" No, he took Jesus at His Word and marched off to Galilee with the other disciples to meet Him. Peter got back up on his feet and got moving again by faith.

We have to do the same thing. We may never have to arise from a fall exactly like Peter's. We may never deny the Lord. In fact, we probably won't. But there are all kinds of falling. There are times when we fall because we look away from Jesus at our circumstances and sink into fear and doubt. Times when we trust our own fleshly strength, depend on logic instead of revelation, and stumble away from the plans of God. There may even be times we plummet because we lose our spiritual passion, start following at a distance, and wind up warming at the wrong fire.

None of those falls are good. They all hurt, and we want with all our hearts to avoid them. But as we're growing up in Jesus, that's not always possible. Sometimes we stumble. Sometimes we slip. If we live in fear of falling, we'll do it more often. Like a novice on a trapeze, our concentration will be interrupted and our faith will be more likely to fail. If we live by faith in God's grace net, the opposite will happen. We'll keep moving upward. Confident that Jesus' arms are outstretched beneath us, we will be far less likely to fall.

Peter spent the rest of his life demonstrating that fact. Once he caught sight of the transforming power of God's grace on the morning of the resurrection, he began to be known more for his boldness than for his blunders. His mess-ups became minor and paled in proportion to the miracle-working power that flowed through him. In the end, he was so confident in his own and every other believer's God-given greatness in Christ, he wrote these eternal words:

"...You are a chosen generation, a royal priesthood, a holy nation, [God's] own special people, that you may proclaim the praises of Him who called you out of darkness into His marvelous light; who once were not a people but are now the people of God, who had not obtained mercy but now have obtained mercy" (1 Peter 2:9-10).

245

Notice, Peter didn't put God's mercy in the future. He didn't say mercy is coming to us one of these days. He said mercy is here now. God has already given it to us through Jesus. That means when we mess up, we don't have to wonder if God will forgive us. His mercy is already ours. All we have to do is come boldly to His throne. "There we will receive his mercy, and we will find grace to help us when we need it."[96]

Because grace and mercy are different, they provide us with a double blessing. Through grace, God gives us good things we don't deserve. Through mercy, He delivers us from the bad things we actually do deserve. We need to grow in our revelation of both so that when Satan tries to inflict on us some kind of punishment and says, "You deserve this, you dirty dog you!" we can shout, "Mercy!" and put him on the run. When he tries to rob us of God's blessings by telling us we don't deserve them, we can shut him up by shouting, "Grace!"

"But Dennis, it's not just the devil who's hounding me about the mistakes I've made," you might say. "People are criticizing me too."

I'm sure they are, and most likely they always will be. Inside the church or out, there's never any shortage of volunteers eager to set themselves up as our judge and jury. But we can ignore them because God hasn't really given them that job. Our heavenly Father is our only Judge and He judges us in Christ. He judges us as washed in the blood of Jesus and made righteous in His sight. He judges

---

[96]Hebrews 4:16 NLT

us not according to our performance, but according to His mercy and grace.

Read 1 Peter 2:9 again in the Wuest translation.

"...But as for you, you are a race chosen out, king-priests, a set-apart nation, a people formed for God's own possession, in order that you might proclaim abroad the excellencies of the One who out of darkness called you into participation in His marvelous light."

God isn't waiting to see if we qualify for greatness. He's already qualified us and called us to participate in His Kingdom at the highest levels. He's already made us kings and priests. As far as He's concerned our place with Him is secure. If we'll believe it and act like it's true, He'll turn even our failures to our advantage. He'll transform us fully as He transformed Peter, deliver us from the fear of falling, and free us by grace to soar into a supernaturally satisfied life.

Dr. Dennis Burke is internationally known as a Bible teacher and bestselling author. For more than 33 years, Dennis has helped thousands discover how to live a victorious life through faith in God's Word. Dennis has been the keynote speaker in churches, conventions, and seminars around the world.

Dennis and his wife Vikki are co-founders of Dennis Burke Ministries in Arlington, Texas. They have one daughter, Jessica Shook. In 2003 Dennis received his Doctorate in Theology from Life Christian University, Tampa, Florida.

They have authored numerous books such as *How to Meditate God's Word* and *Grace — Power Beyond Your Ability* and Vikki's best selling book, *Some Days You Dance.*

BOOKS BY DENNIS BURKE

Dreams Really Do Come True –
It Can Happen to You
Grace: Power Beyond Your Ability
How to Meditate God's Word
Knowing God Intimately
Developing a Winning Attitude
Breaking Financial Barriers
You Can Conquer Life's Conflicts

AUDIO MESSAGES BY DENNIS BURKE

How to Redefine Your Life
Falling into Greatness
The Believer's Rightful Place
Creating an Atmosphere and Attitude for Increase
How to Cast Off Whatever Has Cast You Down
How to bring Your Dreams to Life

BOOKS BY VIKKI BURKE

Some Days You Dance

Aim Your Child Like an Arrow

Relief and Refreshing from Stress

Transforming a Distorted Self-Image

The Power of Peace—
Protection and Direction

AUDIO MESSAGES BY VIKKI BURKE

Pressing through the Promise
into Possession

Burn with Passion—
Reach a Higher Level of Living

Start your day, armed with *the* Truth.

So many will begin their mornings tuning in to TV news, or fill the quiet with the empty banter of early morning secular talk shows. We all know starting off right can prepare us for victory. Why not fuel up with strength-boosting encouragement and insights from God's Word?

Following are just a few testimonies from the growing number of believers who have chosen to brighten their mornings with the light of God's Word through the DBM *Enriching Life Daily* devotional emails:

testimonies

Try *Enriching Life Daily with Vikki Burke!*
DennisBurkeMinistries.org

Insights ....

at home or on the go